BEYOND THE LAKE OF FIRE

James T. Harman

**Prophecy
Countdown
Publications**

BEYOND THE LAKE OF FIRE

Prophecy Countdown Publications
P.O. Box 941612
Maitland, FL 32794
www.ProphecyCountdown.com

Lightning Source
1246 Heil Quaker Blvd.
LaVergne, TN 37086
USA

ISBN: 978-0-9636984-2-1

All references from Scripture are from the King James Version unless noted otherwise: ESV – English Standard Version®, copyright © 2001 Crossway
NAS – New American Standard, copyright © 1960
NLT – New Living Translation, copyright © 1996
NIV – New International Version, copyright © 1973
NKJV- New King James Version, copyright © 1982
YLT – Young's Literal Translation, copyright © 1898

Numerical references to selected words in the text of Scripture are from James H. Strong Dictionaries of the Hebrew and Greek words.

Words in bold emphasis are authors and not in original Scripture. Certain words such as Kingdom and Lake of Fire are capitalized to emphasize their importance, but not in accordance with Traditional fashions.

The picture meant as a depiction of the Lake of Fire on the front cover is titled: *Venus' Once Molten Surface*. Credit: E. De Jong et al. (JPL), MIPL, Magellan Team, NASA. Back cover & Page 13: APOD 1/2/2005 *Welcome to Planet Earth* Credit: Apollo 17 Crew, NASA and APOD 4/23/2010 SDO: *The Extreme Ultraviolet Sun* Credit: NASA / Goddard / SDO AIA Team

Prologue

The picture on the front cover, intended as a representation of the Lake of Fire, is actually a picture of the molten surface of planet Venus taken between: 1990-1994. It can be found at the Astronomy Picture of the Day (APOD) website on 8/1/2010: http://antwrp.gsfc.nasa.gov/apod/ap100801.html.

The Lake of Fire is only mentioned five times in the closing chapters of the book of Revelation and it is not the type of subject most people want to think or talk about. Being cast into the Lake of Fire is not a topic most of humanity wants to consider, so why write a book about such an unpopular subject?

Last year the Lord led me to write my most important book entitled *THE KINGDOM*. I completely expected it to be my last manuscript; however, the Lord had additional purposes in mind. After sharing *THE KINGDOM* with my pastor, he gave it a cold reception – providing little encouragement and a total lack of interest in helping to distribute its vital message to the Church. Because I consider its message to be of utmost importance in this current Laodicean age, I felt the Lord was leading me on to find another place to serve and worship Him.

In my search for a new church home, the Lord introduced me to many new brothers and sisters in Christ. In January I visited a small church that showed a film about the birth of Christ. I was very familiar with the teaching on the video because a man by the name of Ernest L. Martin wrote a book many years ago called: *The Star That Astonished the World.* (Dr. Martin shows that Jesus was born on the Feast of Trumpets in 3 BC, which happened to fall on September 11! The Magi then visited Him when he was a toddler on December 25, 2 BC.)

Watching the film, prompted me to revisit Dr. Martin's great book. Fortunately, I also felt led to Dr. Martin's website where I was astonished to discover all of his additional writings. While I haven't read all of his material and don't necessarily agree with all of his conclusions and terminology, he did introduce me to a subject that I had never encountered throughout my Christian life.

This encounter has led me on a most beautiful journey to discover a doctrine that was taught in the churches for almost 500 years after Christ's departure from planet Earth.

This wonderful doctrine was taught by our Lord Jesus Christ as well as several of His disciples. As you will see later in this book, the Apostle Peter's writings confirm the teaching by Apostle Paul who called this doctrine the *"Glorious Gospel:"*

> *"In whom the god of this world hath blinded the minds of them which believe not, lest the light of the **glorious gospel** of Christ, who is the image of God, should shine unto them."* (II Corinthians 4:4)

> *"According to the **glorious gospel** of the blessed God, which was committed to my trust."* (I Timothy 1:11)

As Paul points out, the god of this world (Satan) has blinded non-believers and the Apostle felt that his ministry was given to him as a sacred trust to proclaim this *"glorious gospel."* Unfortunately, Satan has blinded not only the lost, but also most of the Church. The *"glorious gospel"* entrusted to the Apostles has all but faded away.

The purpose of this book is to help revive this important teaching for the final generation which is about to witness Christ's soon return. But in order to understand this *"glorious gospel"* we will need to go on a journey...a journey that will take us to and then....*Beyond the Lake of Fire.*

Dedication

This book is dedicated to:

- Dr. Ernest L. Martin, whose writings led me to discover the teachings expounded in this short work; and to

- My son Jon who was baptized as a young boy; but as he grew older, rightly rejected many of the false tenets taught from the pulpit; and finally to

- All those who have been turned off by Churches which teach of a God who is fairly different from the one encountered during the first 500 years of the Church.

May this book, in some small measure; help restore the beliefs of the Early Church.

"For the grace of God has appeared bringing salvation to all men." (Titus 2:11 – NAS)

"5) For there is one God and one mediator between God and men, the man Christ Jesus, 6) who gave himself as a ransom for all men..." (I Timothy 2:5-6 – NIV)

"The LORD will demonstrate his holy power before the eyes of all the nations. The ends of the earth will see the salvation of our God." (Isaiah 52:10 – NLT)

Pronouncements

"For so hath the Lord commanded us:

I have set thee for a light of nations** -- for thy being for **Salvation unto the end of the earth."
(Acts 13:47 – YLT)

═══════════════════

"He was the true Light,
Which doth enlighten every man,
Coming to the world."
(John 1:9 – YLT)

═══════════════════

"The Lord says to me,

"It is not enough for you as my servant
To bring the tribes of Jacob back to their land.
It is not enough for you to bring back
The people of Israel I have kept alive.

I will also make you a light for other nations.
Then you will make it possible
For the whole world to be saved."
(Isaiah 49:6 – NIRV)

Table of Contents

Advocates of the *"Glorious Gospel"*[1]

Jesus Christ
The Apostle Paul (I Tim 4:9-11 – "Savior of all mankind")
The Apostle John (John 4:42 – "the Savior of the world")
The Apostle Peter (Acts 3:19-21 and Appendix B)
Clement of Alexandria
Origen
Sir Isaac Newton
Daniel Defoe
Issac Watts
Thomas Gainseborough
Robert and Elizabeth Browning
Robert Burns
Samuel Taylor Coleridge
Emily Bronte
Alexander Pope
William Wadsworth
Ralph Waldo Emerson
Andrew Jukes
Thomas Guthrie
Nathaniel Hawthorne
Hans Christian Anderson
Henry Wadsworth Longfellow
Oliver Wendell Holmes
Alfred Tennyson
Lewis Carroll
Walt Whitman
Victor Hugo
Thomas Carlyle
Abraham Lincoln
Benjamin Franklin
George Washington
Dr. Ernest L. Martin
Ruth Carter Stapleton (President Jimmy Carter's sister)
Charles M. Schultz (cartoonist – Peanuts & Charlie Brown)

Foreword

I was pleased to have received an advance copy of this thought-provoking book by Jim Harman, and believe its readers will be blessed.

Be forewarned! This is not a book you will find in most Christian bookstores, or recommended by most "mainline" Christians. It contains Biblical truths that are missed by church-going Christians who have no desire to think or study for themselves, but who are content to let their pastor, Bible teacher, or mainstream Christian author do their thinking for them.

I would remind the reader before starting the journey through this book, that the apostle Paul was rejected by mainstream Christians! When he made his final return to Jerusalem he was opposed not by unbelieving Israelites, but by those that believed but were zealous for the law. (Acts 21:10) These mainline Christians of their day did not grasp the truths that Paul presented. And we read in Paul's final letters that nearly all had abandoned him.

The apostle Paul found himself in the minority; rejected by "orthodox" believers. Remember that when you talk with your friends about what you read in this book.

That which the author presents is not new. It may seem foreign, as it will challenge the reader beyond the bounds of the preaching and teaching of most churches today. The "*glorious gospel*" that the author refers to is based upon the Bible, aside from the error-filled traditions of men that have infiltrated our churches. But don't take the author's word for anything he says. Search the Scriptures (Acts 17:11) as you read this book. Make every effort to escape the bias of the teachings you have received.

A final warning! Some may read their Bibles and disagree with some of the things the author presents. Keep in mind that no English translation of the Bible is perfect. Most translations use words like *"eternal"* or *"endless,"* but remember these most often come from the Greek *"aion"* in the original manuscripts, from which our English *"eon"* is derived. This is why many translations become very inconsistent, choosing a word like *"age-abiding"* as the context clearly will not support *"endless."* This uncovers a major problem in Bible translations. If *"aion"* were consistently translated *"eon"* or *"age"* all would make perfect sense, and the truth would find its way to the reader. But, alas, we find ourselves subject to bias-filled translators.

The point being: to understand truth, then, we must consult not only the Bible, but also a good concordance that will allow us to check the work of the translator. Young's Analytical Concordance is recommended for this purpose, as it allows the reader to trace back to the original languages as well. And even better, but a bit more difficult to use, is Wigram's "Englishman's Greek Concordance" and its Hebrew counterpart.

Cast off, as much as is possible, the church-teaching bias ... hear what the author has to say ... keep your Bible handy ... and refer also to one of the aforementioned concordances. The author presents these truths in a well organized and easy to understand fashion. I think you will be blessed by what he has to say.

God is so much bigger than mainstream Christianity presents Him to be. The work of Christ will ultimately save and reconcile not just some, but *all* of God's creation – just as He wills. Neither the will of man, nor the will of the Deceiver, can thwart the love, the wisdom and the power of God!

Bob Evely, 9/25/2010
www.GraceEvangel.org

Preface

Before we begin our journey to the Lake of Fire and beyond, it is important to understand some basic terminology. As mentioned in the Prologue, the Apostle Paul used the term *"glorious gospel"* to describe the important doctrine to be addressed in this book.

As pointed out earlier, the *"glorious gospel"* was advocated by Jesus Christ as well as some of His chief Apostles. Also, down through the centuries many famous individuals have been proponents and advocates of this important belief. The Apostle Peter referred to it in the book of Acts when he stated:

> *"19) Repent ye therefore, and be converted, that your sins may be blotted out, when the times of refreshing shall come from the presence of the Lord; 20) And he shall send Jesus Christ, which before was preached unto you: 21) Whom the heaven must receive until the* **times of restitution of all things,** *which God hath spoken by the mouth of all his holy prophets since the world began."* (Acts 3:19-21)

In verse 21, Peter indicates that Jesus has gone back to heaven until the time when He will return for the **"restitution of all things."** The Greek word for restitution is *apokatastasis* (Strong's # 605) which means:

RESTORATION
a) of a true theocracy
b) of the perfect state before the fall

In other words, the Apostle Peter was indicating that there will come a time when Jesus Christ will return to restore the world to that perfect state before the fall of Adam.

It is important to point out that Peter indicates that this is not some new doctrine that he invented. He confirms that all of God's holy prophets since the world began were looking for the time when all things are restored to that perfect state that existed before the fall.

The *"glorious gospel"* that the Apostle Paul had been entrusted to proclaim included the teaching that God's overall plan for mankind is the complete restoration of all things. Yes, Jesus Christ will be returning very soon to restore everything and everyone to that perfect state that existed before Adam fell.

The purpose of this short study is to show what happened to the preaching of the *"glorious gospel"* that was entrusted to the early Apostles. As Satan has blinded the lost to the glorious truth that can be found in Christ Jesus, he has also robbed the Church by depriving us of one of the most beautiful stories to share with the whole world. Satan is the mastermind of deceit and deception and he has succeeded in keeping the truth from most of mankind since the early Church.

HERESY

Down though the centuries, people have attempted to revive its teaching and certain unfortunate labels have been developed to explain the basic doctrine: Universal Reconciliation, Universal Salvation, Christian Universalism, Restorationist, as wells as Universalism (non-biblical). Once such labels are attached to those who hold such different beliefs, most Orthodox Christians will immediately come to the conclusion that these groups must be preaching "heresy" and therefore avoid any and all contact with them. Satan then will have accomplished his objective!

Rather than try to label this important teaching, this writing will use the term **"glorious gospel"** which the Apostle Paul employed to describe the wonderful truth about God's plan to bring about the complete restoration of the world when Jesus Christ returns to planet Earth. It is my hope that the reader will keep an open mind and not jump to the conclusion that this book must be pure heresy. I must admit that when I first read Dr. Martin's writings on this subject I was quite skeptical at first. This teaching goes against everything that I have been taught, particularly since I spent a great deal of time in Baptist churches in my earlier years as a young Christian.

But the more I considered the subject; the Holy Spirit prompted me to continue reading with an open mind. Last year I had just completed my studies for the book *THE KINGDOM* which included such topics as: Outer Darkness, Hell, Sheol, Hades, Tartarus, Gehenna, the Second Death, the Book of Life, etc. Little did I know, but this provided the background that was necessary to prepare me for this current endeavor.

While *THE KINGDOM* is an essential work for the Church to understand, the Lord wants us to look beyond the end of the Millennium and then, even beyond the Lake of Fire:

| Kingdom (Millennial Age) | Great White Throne Judgement Period (**Lake of Fire**) | New Heaven & New Earth (Perfect Age) |

As depicted in the above diagram, this current title will pick up where **THE KINGDOM** left off. Once the Millennial Age or the 1,000 year rule and reign of Jesus Christ has come to an end, the period of the Great White Throne Judgement will begin.

GOOD AND BAD NEWS

This book has the proverbial good news – bad news. The good news is that in God's unending love for mankind He has provided us with the *"glorious gospel"* that Jesus Christ will be returning to bring about the complete restoration of the entire world. The bad news is the fact that the Lake of Fire is still very, very real. The vast majority of mankind will have an encounter with the Lake of Fire if they fail to come into a right relationship with Jesus Christ before they die or before Christ returns. If you have not been born again, then you need to believe on the Lord Jesus Christ for salvation today. Paul put it simply:

> *"..if you confess with your mouth, 'Jesus is Lord,' and believe in your heart God raised him from the dead, you will be saved."* (Romans 10:9 – NIV)
> *"...everyone who calls on the name of the Lord will be saved."* (Romans 10:13 – NIV)

Some have called it "easy believism," but the salvation that Jesus offers is free. Call upon Him now and He will save you. Also, please see the **Special Invitation** at the end of this book.

As stated above, the Lake of Fire is very, very real. While the Lake of Fire can be avoided – being born again is only the first step. Don't put this book down prematurely or you might miss the most important part. We are about to go on an exciting journey that will finally end at a glorious time far, far Beyond the Lake of Fire.

Chapter 1 – Tradition

Paul gives us a strong warning about "Tradition" as shown in the following translations of Colossians 2:8:

> *"Beware lest any man **spoil you** through philosophy and vain deceit, after the **tradition of men**, after the rudiments of the world, and not after Christ."* (KJ)

> *"See to it that no one **takes you captive** through hollow and deceptive philosophy, which depends on **human tradition** and the basic principles of this world rather than on Christ."* (NIV)

> *"See that no one shall be **carrying you away** as spoil **through the philosophy** and **vain deceit,** according to the deliverance of men, according to the rudiments of the world, and not according to Christ."* (YLT)

Tradition is a philosophy created by man through vain deceit and its effect can be to spoil us and to take us captive. It can even carry us away as a spoil!

Paul warns all Christians: *"Study to shew thyself approved unto God, a workman that needeth **not to be ashamed**, **rightly dividing the word of truth**."* (II Timothy 2:15)

Tradition can create a teaching that appears to be correct, but if it has not been *"rightly divided"* then it can cause us to be ashamed.

My wife and I began the ministry of **Prophecy Countdown** back in 1990 to help prepare the Bride of Christ for the return of our wonderful Bridegroom. All of our newsletters and books have been written to encourage the believer in Christ and to force them to dig deep into the Word to see what the Lord is really telling us. Over the years we have uncovered numerous cases where the Church has been duped into believing teachings that are completely contrary to what God meant.

In some of my previous writings I have been ashamed for teaching *"after the tradition of men."* I have since repented of these and asked for forgiveness wherever my previous teachings may have hurt anyone's faith in the Lord or in His Word.

PRE-TRIB RAPTURE

The first major "Tradition" that I had to apologize for was back in 1991. At that time, I had written books on the subject of the Rapture and I strongly believed in the traditional teaching taught by most prophecy teachers. The traditional view says that when Jesus returns, all Christians will be Raptured before the Tribulation period begins. This is the view held by most believers living in the Church today, but sadly it is based upon man's tradition and not what the Word of God has to say.

In 1991, the Lord showed me that not all believers will be taken at first but that there will be a **Separation** between the wise and foolish virgins (Matthew 25:1-10). Those Firstfruit believers who are found in the Church of Philadelphia (and a few of those in Sardis) will be taken to be with the Lord before the Antichrist is revealed. The remaining Lukewarm believers who are found in the Church of Laodicea will be **Left Behind** to face their time of testing.

As a result of shedding the Traditional view, the Lord had us produce the book entitled *THE COMING SPRIITUAL EARTHQUAKE.* A PDF version of this book is available for free by going to our Website: www.ProphecyCountdown.com

"NO ONE KNOWS THE DAY OR HOUR"

The next Tradition that the Lord helped me shed was the one based upon a verse in Matthew:

> *"But of that day and hour knoweth no man, no, not the angels of heaven, but my Father only."* (Matthew 24:36)

The Traditional teaching on this subject says that we are not to know when Jesus will return and we should not concern ourselves with it. This Tradition is also discussed in great detail in the book mentioned above. We are to know when the Lord returns and we should be actively watching for that great day!

"70TH WEEK OF DANIEL"

The Traditional teaching on the 70th Week of Daniel is firmly implanted in the vast majority of Christians today. This teaching has been so engrained in our minds that it is hard to imagine how it could be wrong.

Our book: *DON'T BE LEFT BEHIND* examines this Tradition in detail. It clearly shows that we have been "blinded" to what the Scriptures are really saying. It has taken most of the Church *"captive"* and *"carried us away"* into error that can make us all ashamed for not *"rightly dividing the word of truth."*

THE KINGDOM

The Traditional teaching on the Kingdom has taken the Church captive into believing all Christians will rule and reign with Christ no matter if they have lived faithful and obedient lives, or if they have been slothful and disobedient with the talents God has given them.

The purpose of our latest book: *THE KINGDOM* is to help the Church realize that the Traditional teaching is in error and can be very harmful to the future well being of many Christians. Here again, readers can obtain a free PDF version of this book that is available at our Website: www.ProphecyCountdown.com

ETERNAL TORMENT OF LOST

One of the main purposes of this current book is to bring to light how one of the most fundamental teachings in the Church today has created a doctrine that is completely different from what Jesus and the early Apostles taught. The immediate reaction by most Christians is to say: "Heresy, Heresy! Throw that book away – let's burn it in the fireplace!"

Before you stop here, please ask the Lord to show you what the real truth is. Please keep an open mind, and at least consider the findings in this short work.

Arthur Bloomfield once shared the following insight:

> "The only defense against false teaching is truth…(and)…false doctrine is like a disease germ; it sets up a mental block to truth. A person once infected is very difficult to reach. It seems as if one simply cannot get through to him."[2]

Joseph E. Kirk also related:

> "Far more often than most people realize the traditions and teachings of men are used to invalidate the word of God and are substituted for what God has actually revealed in the Scriptures."[3]

Traditions are created and then handed down as if they are sound biblical doctrine. The Traditional teaching on the eternal torment of the lost is one of Satan's greatest masterpieces.

Breaking from this Traditional teaching is very hard. One wants to hold onto it so dearly because it has been taught so widely that to think otherwise sounds impossible. How could we have so wrongly understood the Scripture?

Without an open mind and teachable spirit, it is next to impossible to allow the Holy Spirit the opportunity to teach us. We can become so steeped in human Tradition, that we can't even hear what God's Word is saying to us. Jesus warned us of this in Mark 7:13:

> *"Thus you nullify the word of God by your tradition that you have handed down. And you do many things like that."* (Mark 7:13 NIV)

Tradition can actually nullify the word of God! The King James version says, *"rendered the Word of God of no effect."* By listening to and by following Tradition, we can entirely miss what God is saying to us in His Word.

Tradition is like spiritual quicksand, pulling all its victims deep into its dark depth. Satan can use Tradition to keep people from the truth of God's Word. This can be extremely dangerous for the Church. We can become so sure of ourselves and of our own position that we actually are led astray to teach doctrine that is completely contrary to what the Scripture says.

EARLY APOSTLES

If the first Apostles were alive today to witness what the Church teaches regarding eternal torment, they would be astonished. Immediately they would ask what became of the sound doctrine that shows Jesus Christ is to return and restore the world to that perfect state before the fall of Adam (Acts 3:21). In the pages that follow we will examine how we have departed from the *"glorious gospel"* which the Apostle Paul proclaimed:

> *"In whom the god of this world hath blinded the minds of them which believe not, lest the light of the **glorious gospel** of Christ, who is the image of God, should shine unto them."* (II Corinthians 4:4)

*"According to the **glorious gospel** of the blessed God, which was committed to my trust."* (I Timothy 1:11)

We believe that the Bible is the inspired Word of God given to mankind to help us in this life and to assist in preparation after we die. We believe it's important not to add or subtract from it:

> *18)....If any man shall add unto these things, God shall add unto him the plagues that are written in this book: 19) And if any man shall take away from the words of the book of this prophecy, God shall take away his part out of the book of life..."* (Revelation 22:18-19)

We will examine how Satan has intervened in the development of the canon of Scriptures in our Bibles through the use of subtle changes based upon man's philosophy of the world instead upon Christ. While we firmly believe the Bible is the inspired Word of God, we will show how Traditions have crept in and translator's biases have helped lead mankind astray.

May we all pray for the Holy Spirit to give us open hearts that are teachable to what He wants to show us. May we be careful not to follow the Traditions of the past if they do not line-up with what the Word of God actually says.

"Dear Lord, give us all the ability to discern what the truth of your Holy Word has to say to us. Give us ears that will listen and hearts that will understand. In Jesus name we pray. Amen."

Glorious Gospel	**Augustinian Tradition**
• Big God	o Small God
• Small devil	o Big Devil
• God's will prevails	o Man's will prevails
• Future glorious for all	o Future tragic for most

(Adapted from **Hope Beyond Hell** by Gerry Beauchemin)[4]

Chapter 2 – Early Church Teachings

We need to preface our remarks by stating that we do not believe in attaching labels to one's belief. We do not necessarily agree with all of the tenets of the various groups who may hold similar views with such titles as: Universal Reconciliation, Universal Salvation, Christian Universalism, Restorationist, etc. We do believe that the early Church had a completely different understanding than today's Church, so this chapter will begin to show how we got to where we are now.

APOSTLE PAUL

We have already seen that Apostle Paul was one of the chief proponents of the *"glorious gospel"* and that Apostle Peter taught Christ will return to bring about the complete restoration of the world as it was before the fall in the Garden of Eden:

> *20) And he shall send Jesus Christ, which before was preached unto you: 21) Whom the heaven must receive until the **times of restitution of all things,** which God hath spoken by the mouth of all his holy prophets since the world began."*(Acts 3:20-21)

The Greek word for restitution is *apokatastasis* (Strong's # 605) which means: RESTORATION a) of a true theocracy and b) of the perfect state before the fall. Apostle Peter was indicating that there will come a time when Jesus Christ will return to restore the world to that perfect state before the fall of Adam.

To understand God's plan for the restoration of mankind, we need to understand what actually took place in the Garden.

> *"21) For since by man came death, by man came also the resurrection of the dead. 22) For as in Adam all die, even so in Christ shall all be made alive."*
> (I Cor.15:21-22)

In his letter to the Corinthians, the Apostle Paul reminds us that death came about through Adam. Because of Adam's disobedience to the word of God, Adam died and caused all mankind to inherit the same condition. Because of Adam's sin, every man will face death (unless the Rapture occurs first).

Paul then tells us the good news that Jesus came to provide for the resurrection of the dead. Whereas all men will die because of Adam, all mankind will be made alive through Christ's victory – the resurrection of the dead. Because of Jesus, **all men will be made alive**.

For further confirmation of the doctrine on the salvation of all men, Paul relates the following:

> *"For therefore we both labor and suffer reproach, because we trust in the living God, who is the **Saviour of all men, <u>specially</u>** of those that believe."*(I Tim. 4:10)

Notice in his letter to Timothy, Paul indicates that Jesus is the Saviour of all men and specially believers. If Paul did not mean to say Jesus saves all men, he would have just said Jesus is the Saviour of believers. But Paul made a point to show the distinction between two groups: all men and believers. Paul used the same term (Strong's #3122) in a similar passage:

> *"As we have therefore opportunity, let us do good unto all men, **<u>especially</u>** (#3122) unto them who are of the household of faith."* (Galatians 6:10)

Here again, Paul was emphasizing that we should do good to all men and **especially** to believers. Had Paul not meant to make a distinction between the two groups: all men and believers, he would not have used the same term again. In both cases, Paul was trying to show a distinction between two groups. So, in his letter to Timothy he clearly says Jesus is the Saviour of **all men**.

Paul believed that Jesus is the Saviour of all men. Notice his comments in his letter to the Colossians:

> *"19) For in him all the fullness of God was pleased to dwell, 20) and through him to* **reconcile to himself all things***, whether on earth or in heaven, making peace by the blood of his cross"* (Colossians 1:19-20 – ESV)

The blood of Jesus Christ will ultimately bring peace to all mankind. Paul believed and taught that in the end, Jesus will restore and reconcile all men. While one man, Adam brought about death, Jesus came to completely restore the world to the perfect state that existed before the fall.

In later chapters we will see further evidence on why the Apostle Paul believed as he did. Additional support will be given to show how Jesus will ultimately bring about the complete restoration of mankind taught by Paul.

APOSTLE JOHN

The Apostle John believed that Jesus is the Saviour of the world. This is shown first in his Gospel:

> *"And said unto the woman, Now we believe, not because of thy saying: for we have heard him ourselves, and know that this is indeed the Christ,* **the Saviour of the world.***"* (John 4:42)

In John's Gospel, he relates how the Samaritans heard Jesus for themselves and therefore believed that He was indeed the Saviour of the world. The Apostle John records the testimony of these Samaritan witnesses who meet Jesus face to face. This is a first hand account of individuals who were fortunate to meet Jesus. John then records, for us, their belief that He is indeed the Saviour of the world.

Also, in John's first letter he affirms that Jesus is the Saviour of the world:

> *"14) And we have seen and do testify that the Father sent the Son to be the **Saviour of the world**. 15) Whosoever shall confess that Jesus is the Son of God, God dwelleth in him, and he in God."* (I John 4:14-15)

Here John testifies that Jesus is indeed to be the Saviour of the world. He then relates that whoever does confess that Jesus is the Son of God has God living in them. It is important to remember that the Scriptures indicate that eventually everyone will confess that Jesus is Lord:

> *"10) That at the name of Jesus every knee should bow, of things in heaven, and things in earth, and **things under the earth**; 11) And that every tongue should **confess that Jesus Christ is Lord**, to the glory of God the Father."* (Philippians 2:10-11)

Please observe that the Apostle Paul indicates that everyone will eventually confess Jesus Christ is Lord. This includes everyone in heaven, everyone in the earth and everyone in Hades (i.e., "*things under the earth*").

At this point the reader may want to review our discussion of Hell in our last book: **THE KINGDOM**. Also, in the chapters to follow, we will take a closer look at the final outcome of those who will be coming out of the earth. The point to notice here is that even those who are under the surface of the earth will eventually be among those who confess that Jesus is Lord.

In his first letter, the Apostle John testifies that Jesus is the Saviour of the world and that God lives in all those who confess Jesus is Lord. Paul's letter to the Philippians confirms even those under the earth will confess Jesus Christ is Lord.

And finally, in the Apocalypse of John he ends the entire Bible with the statement that the grace of the Lord Jesus Christ be with you all:

> *"The grace of our Lord Jesus Christ **be with you all**. Amen".* (Rev 22:21)

John's benediction to the final book of God's word ends with the proclamation of God's marvelous Grace. Some would argue that John's audience for his book is to the Church, so John is just reminding the Church of how wonderful God's grace is. While this may be true, who is to say that God's grace is only for the Church? The Apostle John knew that Jesus came to save the world and while the book of Revelation may be written to the Church, my guess is John was ending his important book by assuring the world of the wonderful grace of our Lord Jesus Christ that is able to save the whole world.

APOSTLE PETER

We have seen that the Apostle Peter taught that Christ will return to bring about the complete restoration of the world. The final canon of Scripture also includes two letters by Peter that address the return of the Lord to bring about a new heaven and earth:

> *"12) Looking for and hasting unto the coming of the day of God, wherein the heavens being on fire shall be dissolved, and the elements shall melt with fervent heat? 13) Nevertheless we, according to his promise, look for new heavens and a new earth, wherein dwelleth righteousness."* (II Peter 3:12-13)

Peter looked for the time when Jesus would return to bring about a new order where righteousness would be the order of the day. Peter mentions that fire will be one of the key elements in the renovation process that God will use to bring about the coming changes. In the chapters that follow, we will see how God will use fire to bring about this restoration of the world.

There is also another book that was widely circulated during the first several hundred years of the Church. It was called *The Apocalypse of Peter*. While it did not get included in the final canon of Scripture that we have in our Bibles, it was widely read in the churches. Because the material in Peter's Apocalypse aligns with some of the tenets in this book, we felt it is important for the reader to be aware of what it teaches.

CANON OF BIBLE

Readers should understand how we arrived at the books that are included in our Bibles. Many of the early Church fathers cited Peter's Apocalypse in their writings: Theophilus of Antioch (180 AD), Clement of Alexandria (before 215 AD), Methodious of Olympus (311 AD), and Macarius Magnes (400 AD). Clement of Alexandria believed that *The Apocalypse of Peter* was part of the Holy Scripture and Methodious of Olympus also believed it was part of the inspired writings.

One of the oldest (last half of second century) New Testament canon lists was the Muratorian Canon. Peter's Apocalypse was included as part of this original canon. In the Canon of Eusebius (311 AD) he listed it as a "spurious book" which meant that while he considered it orthodox, he also did not considered it as part of the canon.

One of the biggest problems surrounding Peter's Apocalypse is that we do not have a complete, error free copy. The Greek version is very fragmentary, but many scholars believe the Ethiopic version is the most complete text that has been preserved. When the final canon of 27 books of our New Testament was accepted in 367 AD, *The Apocalypse of Peter* was **not** included. Even so, copies of this work continued to be

circulated and scholars have found 4th century sermons ascribed
to *The Apocalypse of Peter.*

While Peter's Apocalypse is not part of the final accepted canon
of inspired Scripture, it agrees with Peter's teaching on the
restitution of mankind previously discussed, as well as the
teachings of the Apostles Paul and John as outlined earlier in
this chapter.   Peter's Apocalypse reveals that, in the end, all of
mankind will ultimately be saved.   In it, Peter paints a vivid
account of how God will use fire after the Great White Throne
Judgement to refine and chasten people in the Lake of Fire.

As stated earlier in this book, the good news is that in God's
unending love for mankind He has provided us with the
"glorious gospel" that Jesus Christ will be returning to bring
about the complete restoration of the entire world.   The bad
news is the fact that the Lake of Fire is still very, very real.   The
vast majority of mankind will have an encounter with the Lake
of Fire if they fail to come into a right relationship with Jesus
Christ before they die or before Christ returns.   Peter's dramatic
description of the fiery trials to be endured in the Lake of Fire
should be ample motivation to turn to Jesus Christ for salvation
now, before it is too late!

Even though *The Apocalypse of Peter* is not included in our
Bible, its message does parallel the findings of this book.   It was
read by the early Church and ranked in popularity to the
Apocalypse of John, known as the book of Revelation.   While
Peter describes a journey through the fiery trials in the Lake of
Fire, he also reveals the ultimate Victory that Jesus Christ's
resurrection will provide for the salvation of all mankind.

OTHER CHURCH FATHERS

In addition to several of the Apostles believing in the eventual
salvation of all men, several more of the original Church fathers

advocated man's ultimate salvation. While we should base our doctrine on the word of God, it is beneficial to understand what was taught during the early Church. This book will not go into an in-depth analysis of all the Church fathers. For the student interested in such a study, the Reference Section of this book includes the details on a few recommended sources: Bob Evely's: *"At The End of The Ages...The Abolition of Hell"[5]*, and Mikkel Dahl's: *"Is Hell Eternal?"[6]* have two excellent reviews of what the early Church believed. For a more in-depth study the reader should see **Universalism in the Early Church** by J.W. Hanson © October 1899 or **Ancient History of Universalism** by Hosea Ballou © 1828, 1842, 1872

For purposes of this book, we will review a few of the important believers in God's final restoration of mankind. It is important to note that J.W. Hanson begins the foreword to **Universalism in the Early Church** with the following:

> "The author believes that the following pages show that Universal Restitution was the faith of the early Christians for at least the First Five Hundred Years of the Christian Era."[7]

Hanson's comment is significant. The Church believed in the salvation of all mankind for the first 500 years of its history. Let's see what several of the early Church fathers believed:

ORIGEN (185 to 254 AD)

Origen is probably the most famous supporters of the doctrine on the restoration of all men. He was a well known, respected, and most learned man who believed in man's ultimate salvation:

> "...punishment is always, in God's intention, remedial; God is wholly good and His justice serves no other purpose than His good purpose of bringing all souls back to Himself."[8]

"...for the fire of hell shall, by its torments, purify him whom neither the apostolic doctrine, nor the evangelical word has cleansed; as it is written, *I will thoroughly purify you with fire.* (Isaiah 1:25) But how long, or for how many ages, sinners shall be tormented in this course of purification which is effected by the pain of fire, he only knows to whom the Father hast committed all judgment, and who so loved his creatures that for them he laid aside the form of God, took the form of a servant, and humbled himself unto death, that all men might be saved and come to the knowledge of the truth." (Ballou, page 118)[9]

Origen believed that God would use fire as a remedial instrument in the final salvation of men. This idea that fire is used for refinement and purification is well documented throughout the Bible as we will see later in this book.

GREGORY OF NYSSA (332 to 398 AD)

Gregory of Nyssa was a respected theologian considered very orthodox. He declared the salvation of all men and in commenting on Paul's declaration in Philippians 2:10 that every knee should bow and every tongue should confess the Lordship of Jesus Christ, Gregory stated:

"In this passage is signified, that when evil has been obliterated in the long circuits of the ages, nothing shall be left outside the limits of good; but even from them [all creatures made by God] shall be unanimously uttered the confession of the Lordship of Christ."[10]

He also echoed Origen's sentiments regarding punishment:

"All punishments are means of purification, ordained by divine love to purge rational beings from moral evil, and to restore them back to that communion with God which corresponds to their nature…(Pridgeon, page 287)[11]

Like Origen, Gregory believed that God would use divine chastisement as a means of bringing men back to a right relationship with their Creator.

DIODORE OF TARSUS (370 TO 390 AD)

Diodore of Tarsus was a teacher and also bishop of Jerusalem who believed in the reconciliation of all men to Christ:

> "For the wicked there are punishments, not perpetual, but they are to be tormented for a certain brief period according to the amount of malice in their works. They shall therefore suffer punishment for a short space, but immortal blessedness without end awaits them. The resurrection, therefore, is to be regarded as a blessing not only to the good but also to the evil."[12]

Diodore's comments are similar to other Church fathers who believed that punishments are remedial in nature to bring about the restoration of all men.

THEODORE OF MOPSUESTIA

About the same time as Diodore, Theodore of Mopsuestia (an eminent leader of the Christian university of Antioch) stated:

> "That in the world to come, those who have done evil all of their life long, will be made worthy of the sweetness of the Divine bounty. For never would have Christ have said 'Until thou hast paid the uttermost farthing,' unless it were possible for us to be cleansed when we have paid our debts…Who is so great a fool as to think that so great a blessing [eternal life in Christ] can be to those who let arise [in their hearts] the occasion of endless torment."[13]

One of Theodore of Mopsuestia's pupils known as Theodore the Blessed also wrote:

> "As all men become mortal through Adam, "so shall the whole nature of mankind (all men) follow the Lord Christ, and be made partaker of the Resurrection." (Allin, page 144)[14]

This belief is right in line with the Apostle Paul's teaching to the Church at Corinth:

> *"21) For since by man came death, by man came also the resurrection of the dead. 22) For as in Adam all die, even so in Christ shall all be made alive."*
> (I Corinthians 15:21-22)

JEROME (340 to 420 AD)

Jerome translated the Hebrew and Greek testaments into Latin. He did not believe in the "eternal" damnation of mankind, but the ultimate redemption of all:

> "The nations are gathered to the Judgment, that on them may be poured out all the wrath of the fury of the Lord, and this in pity and with a design to heal...in order that every one may return to the confession of the Lord, that in Jesus' Name every knee may bow, and every tongue may confess that He is Lord. All God's enemies shall perish, not that they cease to exist, but cease to be enemies..." (Phillips, page 43)[15]

Jerome began as a staunch supporter of Origen and his teachings, but lived in the time when the Church was undergoing a great upheaval. J. W. Hanson notes:

> "The great transition from the Christianity of the Apostles to the pseudo-Christianity of the patriarchs and

Emperors – the transformation of Christianity to Churchianity – may be said to have begun with Constantine, at the beginning of the Fourth Century....Pagan principles held by the masses modified and corrupted the religion of Christ; while the worldliness of secular interest derived from the union of church and state, exerted a debasing influence, and the Christianity of...Origen became the church of the popes, of the Inquisition and of the Middle Ages."[16]

With the changes taking place in the Church, Jerome's contemporary Augustine emerged on the scene as a formidable force in opposition to Origen's teachings on the ultimate salvation of all mankind.

AUGUSTINE (354 to 430 AD)

Augustine refuted the teachings on the salvation of all men in writing a small book entitled *"Against the Priscillianists and Origenists."* This book taught the endless torment of the lost and Augustine became the accepted spokesman of his day. Augustine has exerted an enormous influence on what has become orthodox theology that all but squelched the teachings on the ultimate salvation of mankind as taught by the early Church fathers. J.W. Hanson's observations help explain how Paul's *"Glorious Gospel"* with the *"restitution of all things"* was all but silenced until it was revived in the 16th century:

"The Greek fathers exemplified all these qualities, [sweetness and light] and Clement and Origen were ideals of its perfect spirit. But from Augustine downward the Latin reaction...(was to) flee to external authority to avoid the demands of reason, (and) away from the genius of Christianity, until Augustinianism ripened into Popery, and the beautiful system of the Greek fathers was succeeded by the nightmare of the theology of the mediaeval centuries..."[17]

Chapter 3 – Ages (Aion / Aionios)

So how did the teachings of the Early Church fathers get extinguished for centuries? As noted in the last Chapter, the downfall of Christianity began under Constantine with worldly principles corrupting the pure simplicity that is in Christ. Augustine wrote in Latin, and held little mastery of the Greek language. This limitation played a critical role in the development of his theology of eternal punishment of the lost.

Augustine was asked to re-butte the position that punishment of the lost would only be a temporary measure because the Greek word translated as "everlasting" which is *"aionios"* does not mean eternal, but of **limited duration**. Augustine's ignorance of Greek led him to a mistaken understanding of Matthew 25:46 as the basis for his argument.

> *And these shall go away into everlasting (#166) punishment (#2851): but the righteous into life (#2222) eternal (#166).* (Matthew 25:46)

Had Augustine been adept at handling the original Greek, the above verse would have been properly paraphrased to read:

> *"And these shall go away into chastening for an **age**, yet the righteous into eternal life."* (see Question 3, page 73)

Augustine's admission of his lack of competence in handling Greek should have raised red flags. Unfortunately, his faulty exegesis of this one Scripture created a doctrine that erroneously thrusts all of the lost into *"Eternal Torment!"*

With one fell swoop, the course of Christianity has been dreadfully corrupted for centuries. The eternal torment of the lost is the Traditional teaching of practically all of the Church today. To even question this sacred doctrine will immediately cause one to be labeled as a "heretic."

It is important to understand that until Augustine, all of the Church fathers taught that *aionios* punishment was meant to represent chastening for a limited period of time. Augustine was the first one to argue that *aionios* signified endless. John Wesley Hanson observed:

> "Augustine...at first maintained that it always meant thus [*aionios* signified endless], but at length abandoned that ground, and only claimed that it had that meaning sometimes. He 'was very imperfectly acquainted with the Greek language.'"[18]

Hanson's remarks bring incredible light. The Traditional orthodox view that God will torment the lost with eternal punishment was developed by a man who did not even understand the Greek language! Satan has utilized Augustine's error to create his grandest deception since the Garden of Eden. Since Bloomfield reminded us that the only defense against false teaching is the truth, let's look into the real meaning of the terms: *Aion and Aionios.*

AION and AIONIOS

The Greek word *aion* is a noun that can mean 1) period of time or age, 2) for ever, an unbroken age, eternity, or 3) the worlds. It has been translated by 8 different English words: world (35), worlds (2), course (1), eternal (2), end (1), ages (2), ever (30), ever and ever (21).

Clarence Larkin keenly observed that when the word **"age"** is substituted for each of the above usages, it can be seen *"that not our material world is meant but a 'period of time.'"* We will see shortly how Larkin illustrates the usage of these terms in his beautiful Chart entitled *"Ages."* Also, in Appendix C, we have illustrated how substituting the word *"Age"* in several relevant Scriptures can help clarify the proper meaning for the Greek words. This appendix shows that Young's Literal Translation (YLT) and the English Standard Version (ESV) give a much clearer picture than the customary King James using this term.

The Greek word *aionios* is an adjective derived from the root word *aion*. For a representative example of its usage, let's look at Matthew 18:8:

> *"Wherefore if thy hand or thy foot offend thee, cut them off, and cast them from thee: it is better for thee to enter into life halt or maimed, rather than having two hands or two feet to be cast into* **everlasting** *(#166) fire."*
> (Matthew 18:8)

Here, the King James translators used the word "*everlasting*" for the Greek word *aionios* (#166). Pastor Gary Whipple's observation regarding this error is important:

> "It is the opinion of this writer that the translators of the King James Version of the Bible might have mistranslated one important word in Matthew 18:8. This word is the Greek word "aionian," which was mistranslated as *everlasting*, when it should have been properly translated as *age-lasting*, i.e. the messianic age, or kingdom age. If our Lord had wanted us to know that the fire in this verse was everlasting (as it was translated), i.e. perpetual, permanent, and unchangeable, He would have perhaps used the Greek word "aidios," which literally means everlasting…"

Whipple footnotes his comment quoting Dr. J.J. Grisbach's note: "Aoinan. "The adjective form of the word 'aion' [meaning age] cannot rise higher in meaning than the noun [aion] from which it is derived, and must always be governed by it."[19]

Pastor Whipple is not alone in his belief that *aionios* should be rendered to mean a limited period of time. Rev. John Wesley Hanson devotes an entire book to its study. His excellent work is entitled **The Greek Word AION – AIONIOS, Translated Everlasting – Eternal, in the Holy Bible, Shown To Denote Limited Duration.** In the Preface to his book he states:

> "The verbal pivot on which swings the question, Does the Bible teach the doctrine of Endless Punishment? is the word Aion and its derivatives…and he thinks he has conclusively shown that it affords no support whatever to the erroneous doctrine."[20]

It would be profitable for students of the word of God to take the time to read this wonderful book. Hanson clearly demonstrates that the usage of the words Aion and its offshoots were clearly meant to show a period of limited duration. He details how Jesus and the Early Church fathers understood the term to represent chastisement for a period of time and not eternal punishment.

PROOF-TEXT FOR ETERNAL PUNISHMENT

Now let's return to the critical text which is used to "prove" the eternal punishment of the lost:

> *And these shall go away into everlasting (#166) punishment (#2851): but the righteous into life (#2222) eternal (#166).* (Matthew 25:46)

First of all, it is important to understand the context for this statement by our Lord. Matthew 24 and 25, contain the famous Olivet Discourse that Jesus gave to address three classes of people: Jews (Matthew 24:4-31), Christians (Matthew 24:35 to 25:30) and the Gentiles (Matthew 25:31-46). All three classes of people are dealt with in this important teaching by Jesus.

In order to understand our Lord's statement in verse 46, it is imperative to realize who He is speaking to. The reader is encouraged to read the account in Matthew 25:31-46. This is the famous sheep and goat judgement when Jesus returns at the end of the Tribulation period. The sheep and goats represent Gentiles who are saved during the last part of the Tribulation.

The sheep represent saved Gentiles who ministered to the Jewish people during the final part of the Tribulation (also known as the time of Jacob's trouble). Because the sheep were kind and helped the Jewish people, they are given the reward of entering into: *"the kingdom prepared for you from the foundation of the world."* (Matthew 25:34) This represents a judgement of works for the Gentiles and those found faithful (sheep) are richly rewarded by being able to enter into the earthly aspect of the coming Kingdom.

The goats on the other hand represent saved Gentiles who did not help the Jews during the last part of the Tribulation. Because their works were found lacking (they did not feed, clothe, visit, etc) they were chastised.

> *"44)...**Lord**, when saw we thee an hungred, or athirst, or a stranger, or naked, or sick, or in prison, and did not minister unto thee? 45) Then shall he answer them, saying, Verily I say unto you, In as much as ye did it not to one of the least of these, ye did it not to me. 46) And these shall go away into everlasting (#166) punishment: but the righteous into life eternal."* (Matthew 25:44-46)

Please notice these are saved Gentiles (verse 44, shows they called Him Lord – II Corinthians 12:3). But because of their lack of concern for the Jewish people, they are sent away for punishment for the Kingdom age. The use of *aionios* (#166) by Jesus shows that this period of chastisement or punishment will only last for a limited time. Had Jesus meant to convey this to be eternal punishment, He would have used a different Greek word such as *"aidios"* if it were to be everlasting.

It is vital to understand that the sheep and goat judgement does represent Gentiles **saved** during the last part of the Tribulation. Those found faithfully helping the Jewish people (sheep) will be richly rewarded by entering the coming Kingdom for the 1,000 year reign of the earth. Those who did not help the Jews (goats) will be chastised during this period, but they will not be assigned to eternal punishment.

This judgement is similar to the one that will take place when Jesus comes to judge the Church. At the Judgement Seat of Christ, the faithful overcomers will be richly rewarded by being granted entrance into the coming millennial Kingdom where they will rule and reign with Christ for 1,000 years. However, the unfaithful Christians who were not overcomers will be assigned to Outer Darkness for the same period of time. Please see our last book entitled *THE KINGDOM* for all the details.

In like manner the judgement of the sheep and goats is a separation of saved Gentiles based upon their works. While the faithful sheep are rewarded, the goats are chastised – but certainly **not** assigned to eternal punishment. The doctrine of *eternal punishment* completely falls apart when the principal proof-text is properly examined and interpreted. To assign saved Gentiles to eternal punishment is utterly absurd and totally contrary to God's character.

GOD'S AGES

Now that we see God does not plan to punish the lost for eternity, we need to understand what His overall plan for man actually is. Clarence Larkin's Chart on page 40 shows God has designed five to six key Ages in His purposes for man. The Scriptures delineate these Ages in ways that are seen differently depending upon one's dispensational view.

The Jews see 2 Ages and Post-Millennialist only see 3 Ages in God's plan for mankind. Those who hold a Pre-Millennial view see the Ages more in line with the way God sees them.

PRE-MILLENNIAL VIEW

The Ages begin with Eternity Past, followed by the 1st Age or the **Creative Age** (John 1:1-3, Hebrews 1:2, & II Peter 3:5-6).

The 2nd Age began in the Garden of Eden with the **Age of Conscience**, also known as the Antediluvian Age (the Age before the Flood) and ends with the Flood.

The 3rd Age is the **Present Age** that began after the Flood and goes until Christ returns (I Thessalonians 4:13 – 5:11 and Matthew 24 & 25). Some may want to divide the current Present Age into the Age of Law and the Church Age in which case there are 6 Ages and not 5 Ages.

The 4th and 5th Ages are also referred to as the **Age of the Ages** or the Kingdom of the Son of Man (Ephesians 3:21 and Revelation 11:15).

The 4th Age will be ushered in after the battle of Armageddon and Christ returns to set-up His glorious Kingdom for the 1,000 year reign also known as the **Millennial Age** or **Kingdom Age** (Revelation 20:1-10). The Kingdom Age begins after the Judgement Seat of Christ and the Judgement of the Sheep and the Goats.

The 5th Age is also known as the **Perfect Age** (II Peter 3:13 and Revelation 21:1-2). The 5th Age begins at the Great White Throne Judgement period in which God judges mankind and the earth with Fire.

The 5th Age ends when Jesus Christ turns over the **Perfect Age** to the Father so God may be All in all (I Corinthians 15:24-28).

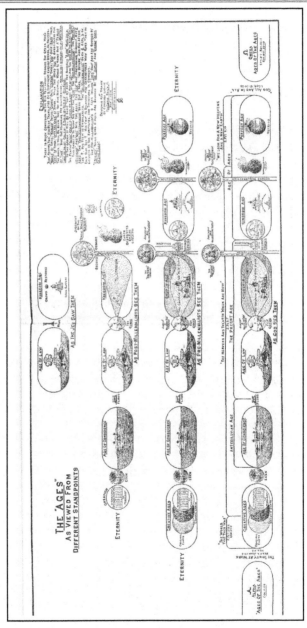

The above Chart is from *Dispensational Truth*, by Clarence Larkin, page 3 ½, © 1918. Used with permission of the Rev. Clarence Larkin Estate, P.O. Box 334, Glenside, PA 19038, U.S.A., 215-576-5590, *www.larkinestate.com*

What Larkin's Chart brings to light is the fact there are at least two more Ages to come once the **Present Age** ends. The current Church Age will draw to a close once the Second Coming of Christ takes place.

The Second Coming will include the Rapture of Firstfruit believers (Rev. 3:8, 12:5, 14:1, II Thess. 2:3 and Luke 21:36) before the Antichrist is revealed followed by the Main Harvest Rapture (Rev. 7:14) after which God pours out His wrath (Rev. 16). It will be followed by the First Resurrection and the Judgement of Christians and Gentiles mentioned previously.

At this point Jesus will begin His reign for at least 2 more Ages:

> *"And the seventh messenger did sound, and there came great voices in the heaven, saying, `The kingdoms of the world did become those of our Lord and of His Christ, and he shall reign to **the ages of the ages**!"*
> (Revelation 11:15 – YLT)

Here we can see that Jesus Christ will begin His Millennial reign also known as the **Kingdom Age** for 1,000 glorious years (Revelation 20:1-6) that will be followed by the **Perfect Age** with a new Heaven and a new Earth (Revelation 21and 22, and II Peter 3:13). Jesus will actually reign over 2 Ages before He finally turns control back to God

> *"Now when all things are made subject to Him, then the Son Himself will also be subject to Him who put all things under Him, that God may be all in all."*
> (I Corinthians 15:28 – NKJV)

The Chart on the following page is an enlargement of the right portion of the Chart found on page 40. It provides the reader with better detail of all the glorious truths that God has in store for the upcoming Ages.

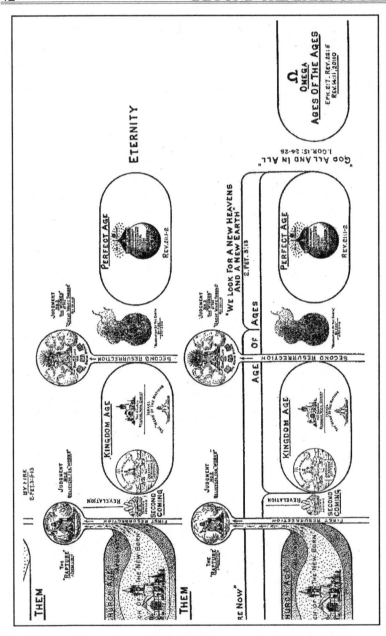

The above Chart is from *Dispensational Truth*, by Clarence Larkin, page 3 ½, Enlarged Section © 1918. Used with permission of the Rev. Clarence Larkin Estate, P.O. Box 334, Glenside, PA 19038, U.S.A., 215-576-5590, *www.larkinestate.com*

Chapter 4 – Death

In order to understand what God has planned for mankind in the Ages to come, we need to go back to the very beginning when God created man in the first place.

The account recorded in the book of Genesis shows that God created mankind in His image to have dominion over the earth. God also gave man specific instructions:

> *"16) And the LORD God commanded the man, saying, Of every tree of the garden thou mayest freely eat: 17) But of the tree of the knowledge of good and evil, thou shalt not eat of it: for in the day that thou eatest thereof thou shalt surely die."* (Genesis 2:16-17)

While man was given dominion over the earth, he was told not to eat from the tree of knowledge of good and evil. Most know the story of how the serpent beguiled Eve who then ate from the tree they were told not to eat. Because of man's disobedience to God, death was the result:

> *"19) ... till thou **return unto the ground**; for out of it wast thou taken: for **dust thou art**, and unto **dust shalt thou return.**"* (Genesis 3:19)

Death then, is a return of the body back to the dust of the ground from which God fashioned him. Not only did Adam's disobedience bring death, it also brought about banishment from the Garden of Eden:

> *22) And the LORD God said, Behold, the man is become as one of us, to know good and evil: and now, lest he put forth his hand, and take also of the tree of life, and eat, and live for ever: 23) Therefore the LORD God **sent him***

> *forth from the garden of Eden, to till the ground from whence he was taken. 24) So he drove out the man; and he placed at the east of the garden of Eden Cherubims, and a flaming sword which turned every way, to keep the way of the tree of life. "* (Genesis 3:22-34)

God originally created man to live and have dominion over everything that He provided in the beautiful paradise called Eden. If Adam and Eve had obeyed, they would have enjoyed living in God's beautiful land and presence for the ages. God needed to keep disobedient man away from the tree of life so He placed Angels and a flaming sword to guard it. God did not want rebellious man to rule any longer in His realm.

THREE PARTS OF MAN

We need to remember that man's nature is made up of three parts: spirit, soul and body. This truth is brought out by Paul in his letter to the Thessalonians:

> *"...and I pray God your whole **spirit** and **soul** and **body** be preserved blameless unto the coming of our Lord Jesus Christ. "* (I Thessalonians 5:23)

Paul prayed for each of the three parts of man. Each is distinct and each has its own destiny when man dies. As we have seen above, when man dies the **body** returns to the **earth**. The body was made out of dust and returns to the dust where it is buried. The spirit of man came directly from the breath of God:

> *"...the Lord God formed the man of dust from the ground and **breathed into his nostrils the breath of life**, and the man became a living creature. "* (Gen.2:7 – ESV)

When man dies, his **spirit** returns to **God**:

> *5) For man is going unto his home age-during (abiding) And the mourners have gone round through the street....*

7) And the dust returneth to the earth as it was, And the **spirit returneth to God who gave it.** *"*
(Ecclesiastes 12:5 & 7 – YLT)

For confirmation of where the spirit goes at death, Jesus told us from the cross:

*"... Jesus, calling out with a loud voice, said, '***Father, into your hands I commit my spirit!***' And having said this he breathed his last. "*(Luke 23:46 – ESV)

The destination of the body and the spirit is fairly simple to understand. The body returns to the earth and the spirit returns to God. The final destination of the soul is a little more difficult to explain and to comprehend.

The **soul** of man represents who we are as a person. It represents our mind, will, and emotions, as well as our intellect and personality. The **spirit** of man connects us to God, the **body** links us to others and the world around us, and the **soul** is the natural part of man that joins the body and spirit into one distinct and unique individual.

REDEMPTION

Because of Adam's disobedience, God sent His son Jesus Christ to redeem mankind from the curse of death. Jesus died for the sins of the entire world so that man could be restored to his former state in the Garden of Eden. In order for man to be completely redeemed, all three parts of man need to be addressed.

The **salvation** of a person's **spirit** is by faith and completely free. It cannot be earned by any works or striving:

"For by grace are ye saved through faith; and that not of yourselves: it is the gift of God: Not of works, lest any man should boast. " (Ephesians 2:8-9)

The salvation of the spirit is 100% free. There is nothing anyone can do in order to earn it, and nothing anyone can do in order to lose it. Once a person is saved, his spirit can never be lost again because it is saved by the gracious gift of God. That person's spirit is guaranteed to be with God for eternity.

The **salvation** of the **soul** is conditional and based upon one's obedience to the word of God. As Adam's disobedience resulted in death, so man's continued disobedience can bring death to the soul:

> "4) *The **soul who sins** is the one who **will die**....*"
> "*9) He follows my decrees and faithfully keeps my laws. That man is **righteous**; he **will surely live**, declares the Sovereign LORD. 19)...Since the son has done what is just and right and has been careful to keep all my decrees, he **will surely live**. 20) **The soul who sins is the one who will die**.*" (Ezekiel 18:4, 9, 19 & 20)

This is saying that the righteous man faithfully keeps all of Gods decrees and will therefore live because of his obedience. The **salvation** of the **soul** is the result of obedience, but the soul who sins will die.

While the **spirit** returns to God and the **body** goes to the earth when it dies, the **soul** that dies goes to *sheol* or *hades* as seen at the death of our Lord:

> "*For You will not leave my soul in **Sheol**, Nor will You allow Your Holy One to see corruption.*" (Psalm 16:10)
> "*For You will not leave my soul in **Hades**, Nor will You allow Your Holy One to see corruption.*" (Acts 2:27)

The Old Testament term *Sheol* is the same place as the New Testament term *Hades*. Both represent the unseen destination of the soul that dies. The righteous will surely live, but the *"soul who sins...will die."*

God's original purpose was to have man live and enjoy living with Him in the beautiful Paradise He had created. But because of disobedience, all mankind faces death:

> *"And just as it is appointed for man to die once, and after that comes judgment,"* (Hebrews 9:27 – ESV)

God's ultimate purpose is to restore mankind to the perfect state that existed before Adam sinned. In order to accomplish this, He has also set in place various judgements to bring man back into a right relationship.   God's first Judgement took place at Calvary where Jesus took upon Himself the sin of the entire world. By shedding His blood, He provided for mankind's redemption.

> *"For the life of the flesh is in the blood: and I have given it to you upon the altar to make an atonement for your souls: for it is the **blood** that maketh an **atonement for the soul.**"* (Leviticus 17:11)

Christ's sacrifice on the cross was the ultimate love gift to man in order to bring about his restoration. By shedding His blood for us, every man will eventually be made alive:

> *"21) For since by man came death, by man came also the resurrection of the dead. 22) For as in Adam all die, even so in Christ shall all be made alive."*
> (I Cor.15:21-22)

Christ's resurrection paved the way for everyone's resurrection. When a person will be resurrected is dependent upon which Judgement they will face.

In order to ensure that all sin, rebellion and disobedience have ended, God has designed two primary judgements. The first one is known as the **Judgement Seat of Christ** and the next one is called the **Great White Throne Judgement** (please see the Charts on Page 42 and Page 50).

JUDGEMENT SEAT OF CHRIST

The Judgement Seat of Christ is a Judgement of the works of those who have been *"born again."* Since all people who appear before this Judgement are believers, the Lord will use this time to reward all those who have been faithful overcomers and to punish those who have been slothful, disobedient and unfaithful. For a complete discussion of this important topic, please see our last book: *THE KINGDOM* that is available for FREE on our website: www.ProphecyCountdown.com

The Judgment Seat of Christ will judge the Christian's works:

> *"For **we must all appear before the judgement seat of Christ**; that every one may receive the things done in his body, according to that he hath done, whether it be **good or bad.**"* (II Corinthians 5:10)

Also, both the good and bad that we do will be **judged by fire**:

> *"Now if any man build upon this foundation gold, silver, precious stones, wood, hay, stubble; Every man's work shall be made manifest: for the day shall declare it, because it shall be revealed by fire; and the **fire shall try every man's work** of what sort it is. If any man's work abide which he hath built thereupon, he shall receive a reward. If any man's work shall be burned, he shall suffer loss: but he himself shall be saved; **yet so as by fire.**"* (I Corinthians 3:12-15)

Paul's letter to the Corinthians shows that our works will be tested by **fire** to determine whether they will stand. Works of gold, silver and precious stones will pass through the flames and result in great reward for the believer. However, works of wood, hay and stubble will be destroyed by these same flames. While Paul warns that the believer will suffer loss of reward, he notes they will still be saved.

The Christian whose works are destroyed by fire will suffer great loss, and thereby lose the opportunity of ruling and reigning with Christ in the Kingdom. Unfortunately, as we will see shortly, even some Christian's will have their part in the Lake of Fire.

GREAT WHITE THRONE JUDGEMENT

The last Judgement that God will use to restore the rest of mankind is known as the Great White Throne Judgement. It will take place at the very end of the 1,000 year Kingdom Age.

> *"11) Then I saw a **great white throne** and him who was seated on it. From his presence earth and sky fled away, and no place was found for them. 12) And I saw the dead, great and small, standing before the throne, and books were opened. Then another book was opened, which is the book of life. And the dead were judged by what was written in the books, according to what they had done."* (Revelation 20:11-12 – ESV)

Whereas the Judgement Seat of Christ judges the works of believers, the Great White Throne Judgment will judge the works of the rest of mankind. As Jesus will use fire to test the works of Christians at their Judgement, fire will also be used to judge humanity at the Great White Throne Judgement:

> *"7) But by the same word the heavens and earth that now exist are stored up for **fire**, being kept until the day of judgment and destruction of the ungodly."*
> (II Peter 3:7 – ESV)

In the following Chapters we will see how God will utilize these upcoming Judgements to fully restore man back to the perfect state that existed before the fall. God loves all men and wants to bring about complete restoration. The Chart on the next page depicts these approaching Judgements to aid in understanding God's magnificent design.

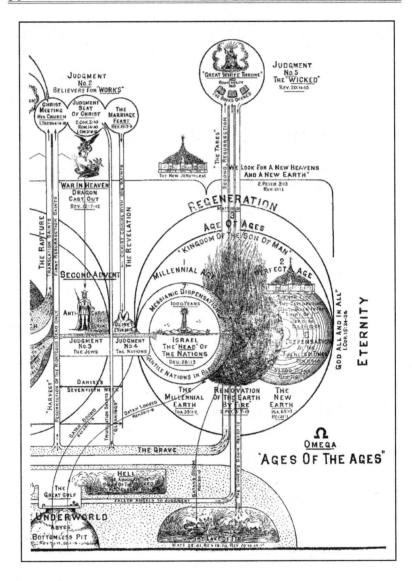

God's Magnificent Plan to Restore Mankind

The above Chart is an enlarged section from *Dispensational Truth*, by Clarence Larkin, right half of page 17 ½, © 1918. Used with permission of the Rev. Clarence Larkin Estate, P.O. Box 334, Glenside, PA 19038, U.S.A., 215-576-5590, *www.larkinestate.com*

Chapter 5 – Lake of Fire

The Lake of Fire is referred to five times in the book of Revelation. The first two times it is mentioned is in relationship to the judgement of the unholy trio: Antichrist (beast), False Prophet, and Satan:

> *"19) Then the **beast** was captured, and with him the **false prophet** who worked signs in his presence, by which he deceived those who received the mark of the beast and those who worshiped his image. These two were cast alive into the **lake of fire** burning with brimstone."* (Revelation 19:20 – NKJV)

> *"20) and the **Devil**, who is leading them astray, was cast into the **lake of fire** and brimstone, where are the beast and the false prophet, and they shall be tormented day and night -- to the ages of the ages."*
> (Revelation 20:10 – YLT)

In the first reference we see the Antichrist and the False Prophet thrown into the Lake of Fire alive. This indicates that these are actually two different human beings who will deceive many in the upcoming Tribulation period. These two deceitful people will arrive on the scene in the very near future to throw this world into chaos like never before seen. Because of this, God will cast both of these individuals alive into the Lake of Fire just before the Kingdom Age begins.

Immediately after the Antichrist and the False Prophet are cast into the Lake of Fire, Satan will be bound for 1,000 years:

> *"2)... Satan, and bound him a thousand years, 3) And cast him into the bottomless pit, and shut him up, and set a seal upon him, that he should deceive the nations no more, till the thousand years should be fulfilled: and after that he must be loosed a little season.* (Rev 20:2-3)

During the 1,000 year Kingdom Age, the Antichirst and the False Prophet will be in the Lake of Fire while Satan will be bound in the bottomless pit. Once the 1,000 years are ended, Satan is released for a *"little season"* at which time he deceives the nations once again (Rev. 20:7-9). Immediately thereafter, Satan is finally cast into the Lake of Fire (Rev. 20:10 – above).

In the second reference to the Lake of Fire, the Apostle John sheds light on its purpose. He says that Satan is cast into the lake where the Antichrist and False Prophet are *"and they shall be tormented day and night -- to the ages of the ages."*

Here we see the initial purpose for the Lake of Fire is to torment this unholy trio for the *"ages of the ages."* This tells us that there are at least two ages involved in their judgement. During the first age – also known as the Millennial Age or Kingdom Age – the Lake of Fire holds the Antichrist and the False Prophet. In the age following the Millennium, Satan will then join them for an additional age of punishment and torment.

LOCATION OF LAKE OF FIRE

Immediately after Satan is cast into the Lake of Fire, John introduces the subject of the Great White Throne Judgement that was mentioned in our last Chapter (page 49). Before we look into the last three references for the Lake of Fire found in the book of Revelation, it would be helpful to understand where this infamous lake is actually located.

What may come as a big surprise to most people, the Lake of Fire was once actively spewing forth smoke and fire. *The Lake of Fire: Where Is it Located?* by Ernest L. Martin, PhD, does an excellent job of explaining that the Dead Sea is actually the location of the Lake of Fire. While it is currently dormant, the Bible indicates it will be re-ignited in the very near future (Rev. 19:20). The map on the facing page shows its location where God will once again use "fire" in the judgements to come.

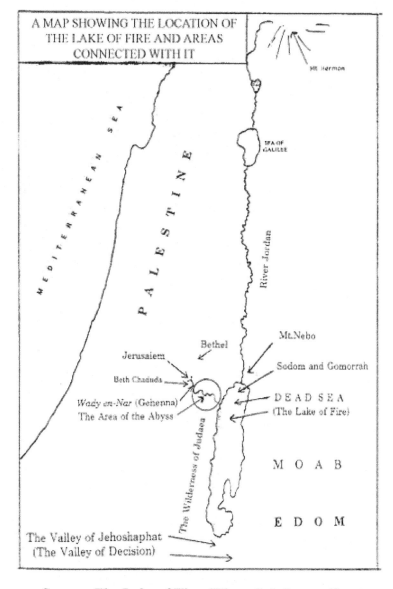

Source: *The Lake of Fire: Where Is it Located?*
By Ernest L. Martin, Ph.D., 1981
Edited by David Sielaff, February 2010
Please see: www.askelm.com/prophecy/p100201.htm

DURATION OF COMING AGES

Now that we know where the coming judgements will be, let's see how long they will last. We know that the first age, called the Kingdom Age, will last for 1,000 years:

> *"4) and they lived and reigned with Christ a thousand years."* (Revelation 20:4)

The Apostle Peter sheds some light on how long the period of judgment following the Kingdom Age will last, and even tells us not to be ignorant regarding this important subject:

> *7) But the heavens and the earth, which are now, by the same word are kept in store, reserved unto **fire** against **the day of judgment** and perdition of ungodly men. 8) But, beloved, be not ignorant of this one thing, that **one day** is with the Lord as **a thousand years**, and a thousand years as one day."* (II Peter 3:7-8)

Peter states the *"day of judgment"* (i.e. Great White Throne) will last for 1,000 years. The Great White Throne Judgement that Apostle John mentions in Revelation is the same one that Peter refers to as *"the day of judgment."* The Great White Throne Judgement <u>period</u> will therefore last for 1,000 years.

GREAT WHITE THRONE

Immediately after Satan is cast into the Lake of Fire, John begins the topic of the Great White Throne Judgement:

> *"11) Then I saw a **great white throne** and Him who sat upon it, from whose presence earth and heaven fled away, and no place was found for them. 12) And I saw the dead, the great and the small, standing before the throne..."* (Revelation 20:11-12 – NAS)

Notice that John says that heaven and earth fled away from Christ's presence when He takes the throne to begin His Judgement. The reason for this is because God ends the Kingdom Age by bringing down fire from Heaven to consume Satan's attacking armies (Rev 20:7). With the completion of the 1,000 years through a fiery judgement, God then ushers in the final age with a new heaven and a new earth:

> *"And I saw a new heaven and a new earth: for the first heaven and the first earth were passed away; and there was no more sea."* (Revelation 21:1)

The Great White Throne Judgement period begins the final Perfect Age. The old heaven and earth have fled away and God inaugurates the remaining 1,000 years with a new heaven and a new earth. The following diagram may be helpful in understanding the order of events and the length of the ages to come:

Kingdom (Millennial Age)	Great White Throne Judgement Period	New Heaven & New Earth
1,000 Years	**(Lake of Fire)**	(Perfect Age)

(One Thousand Years)

With the Kingdom Age completed and the start of the Great White Throne Judgement period we will now look at the final three references to the Lake of Fire.

> *"11) And I saw a **great white throne**, and him that sat on it, from whose face the earth and the heaven fled away; and there was found no place for them. 12) And I saw the dead, small and great, stand before God; and the books were opened: and another book was opened, which is the book of life: and **the dead were judged** out of those things which were written in the books, **according to their works**. 13) And the sea gave up the dead which were in it; and death and hell delivered up the dead which were in them: and **they were judged every man according to their works**. 14) And death and hell were cast into the **lake of fire**. This is the second death. 15) And whosoever was not found written in the book of life was cast into the **lake of fire**."*
> (Revelation 20:11-15)

The above narrative by John gives us two more references to the Lake of Fire. The final mention of this term is found in Revelation 21:8, which will be addressed very shortly.

In John's vision he sees multitudes of people standing before a Great White Throne. He says they are *"the dead"* which means God raised everyone who remained in their graves. The First Resurrection had already taken place 1,000 years earlier (Revelation 20:4), so this is the Second and final Resurrection of the dead.

John says that the sea gave up the dead and that hell gave up the dead which were in them. The term for *"**hell**"* here is *"**hades**"* and the reader will recall from Chapter 4, this is the destination for the soul that dies in sin. Remember that the *"righteous will surely live,"* but the *"soul who sins...will die."*

In other words, all those who are standing before Christ at the Great White Throne represent everyone who has lived and died without Jesus Christ as their Lord and Savior. This is the Second Resurrection and it includes everyone who either rejected Christ or who never heard about Him. Because their names were not found written in the book of life, they were cast into the Lake of Fire.

Before we look at the final place the Lake of Fire is mentioned in the Bible, it is important to take note of one important fact that John brought out in discussing the Lake of Fire. Notice in verse 14, he says: "*And death and hell were cast into the lake of fire. This is the second death.*" When the Antichrist, the False Prophet and Satan are cast into the Lake of Fire, no mention is made of the "*second death.*" But after the Great White Throne Judgement commences and the dead are cast into the Lake of Fire, it also becomes known as the "second death." The next Chapter will discuss this critical topic in detail.

The final time the Lake of Fire is used is found in Chapter 21 of the book of Revelation in verse 8:

> "*5) And he that sat upon the throne said, Behold, I make all things new. And he said unto me, Write: for these words are true and faithful. 6) And he said unto me, It is done. I am Alpha and Omega, the beginning and the end. I will give unto him that is athirst of the fountain of the water of life freely. 7) He that overcometh shall inherit all things; and I will be his God, and he shall be my son. 8) But the fearful, and unbelieving, and the abominable, and murderers, and whoremongers, and sorcerers, and idolaters, and all liars, **shall have their part in the lake which burneth with fire and brimstone: which is the second death.**"* (Revelation 21:5-8)

Chapter 21 deals with the New Jerusalem, but verses 5-8 are a parenthetical statement as a warning to the churches about being an overcomer. Verse 7 says that the overcomer: *"shall inherit all things; and I will be his God, and he shall be my son."* But then verse 8 describes the unfaithful Christian who is not an overcomer. Those believers who are disobedient *"**shall have their part in the lake which burneth with fire and brimstone: which is the second death.**"*

This is a somber warning that Christians need to be aware of as we approach the soon return of our Lord and Saviour Jesus Christ. In Christ's earlier warning to the Church of Smyrna He said:

> *"He that hath an ear, let him hear what the Spirit saith unto the churches; He that **overcometh** shall **not be hurt of the second death.** "* (Revelation 2:11)

Jesus is telling us that overcomers will not be hurt by the second death. The converse of this is that Christians **will be** hurt by the second death if they fail to be overcomers. This is an extremely serious warning that believers need to heed.

Being a faithful, obedient overcomer is vital to a Christian's well being. In the following Chapter we will delve further into the subject of the "second death" and see how God will utilize the Lake of Fire to restore the rest of mankind.

Chapter 6 – Second Death

Ever since the Garden of Eden, Satan has been allowed to roam the earth as a thief in order to kill, steal and destroy (John 10:10). His influence led to man's disobedience which led to sin. And when sin ran its full course, it led to death.

Shortly after the Millennium ends, Satan and all of his evil cohorts will be gone (Rev. 20:3 & 10). They all will have been cast into the Lake of Fire and no longer be around to manipulate mankind. The chief instigator of sin and death will have vanished from the scene, and the "good shepherd" will be sitting on the throne ruling a new heaven and a new earth.

We need to remember that death came as a result of Adam's disobedience, but the good news is that Jesus Christ came to conquer death through His resurrection:

> *"21) For since by man came death, by man came also the resurrection of the dead. 22) For as in Adam all die, even so in Christ **shall all be made alive.**"*
> (I Cor.15:21-22)

All authority was given to Christ and He has the power to cause all mankind to be made alive. At the Great White Throne, billions upon billions of people will be standing before Jesus. Over the span of a thousand years, He will judge each individual with the ultimate purpose of restoring every one to the condition before the fall (Acts 3:21). Each will experience the "second death" of being cast into the Lake of Fire.

LAKE OF FIRE

> *14) And death and hell were cast into the **lake of fire**. This is the **second death**. 15) And whosoever was not found written in the book of life was cast into the **lake of fire.**"* (Revelation 20:14-15)

The "second death" represents being cast into the Lake of Fire. The Greek word for Fire (#4442) is *pur*, from which we get the words purify and purge. God's purpose of using fire is to purge every last trace of disobedience and sin and cleans all of mankind. His chief intention is to purify and restore men to abide in righteousness.

The Scriptures give us several examples of how God uses fire for good:

> *"2) But who can endure the day of His coming? And who can stand when He appears? For He is like a **refiner's fire** And like launderers' soap. 3) He will sit as a refiner and a purifier of silver; He will purify the sons of Levi, And **purge them** as gold and silver, That they may offer to the LORD An offering in righteousness."* (Malachi 3:2-3 – NKJV)

> *"And I will put this third **into the fire, and refine them** as one refines silver, and **test them as gold** is tested. They will call upon my name, and I will answer them. I will say, 'They are my people'; and they will say, 'The Lord is my God."* (Zechariah 13:9 – ESV)

> *"When you pass through the waters, I will be with you; and through the rivers, they shall not overwhelm you; **when you walk through fire you shall not be burned, and the flame shall not consume you.**"* (Isaiah 43:2 – ESV)

Jesus will use the Lake of Fire to refine and purge mankind. The ultimate purpose is to purify each person so they may learn righteousness and obedience. The fire will not consume them and they will not be burned in the flames.

An excellent example of how God used fire without harming the individuals in the flames is the story in Daniel 3.

"16) Shadrach, Meshach and Abednego replied to the king, "O Nebuchadnezzar, we do not need to defend ourselves before you in this matter. 17) **If we are thrown into the blazing furnace, the God we serve is able to save us from it,** *and he will rescue us from your hand, O king.*

"24) **Weren't there three men** *that we tied up and* **threw into the fire?"** *They replied, "Certainly, O king." 25) He said, "Look!* **I see four men walking around in the fire,** *unbound and unharmed, and the fourth looks like a son of the gods."*

27)...and the satraps, prefects, governors and royal advisers crowded around them. They saw that **the fire had not harmed their bodies,** *nor was a hair of their heads singed; their robes were not scorched, and there was no smell of fire on them."*
(Daniel 3:16-17,24-25& 27 – NIV)

Most are familiar with this Bible story where Shadrach, Meshach and Abednego are seen walking in the fire of a blazing furnace. The fourth man in the flames represents Jesus, who is with the three men. He insures that their bodies are not harmed and they are able to pass through the fire.

God is able to deliver men from the fire and He will use the Lake of Fire to redeem mankind. It is important to remember that the Scriptures indicate that eventually everyone will confess that Jesus is Lord:

"10) That at the name of Jesus every knee should bow, of things in heaven, and things in earth, and **things under the earth;** *11) And that every tongue should* **confess that Jesus Christ is Lord,** *to the glory of God the Father."* (Philippians 2:10-11)

The Apostle Paul reminds us that eventually, everyone will confess that Jesus Christ is Lord. This includes everyone in heaven, everyone in the earth, and everyone in Hades, i.e. (*"things under the earth"*). Everyone in Hades will be resurrected before the Great White Throne and then tried in the Lake of Fire from which they will finally confess that Jesus Christ is Lord.

GODLY PUNISHMENT

At this point it is important to realize that while God can and will deliver mankind from the Lake of Fire, it does represent a punishment that will not be pleasant.

> *"...then the Lord knows how to deliver the godly out of temptations and to reserve the unjust under punishment (# 2849) for the day of judgment."* (II Peter 2:9)

The word for punishment is *"kolazō"* # 2849, which can mean:
1) to lop or prune, as trees and wings 2) to curb, check, restrain 3) to chastise, correct, punishment   4) to cause to be punished

While the punishment by God in the Lake of Fire is meant to chasten and correct, it will be a judgement and pruning of all that is evil and sinful. Some will experience mild correction, however, those who had committed heinous crimes such as murder and rape will be forced to endure greater suffering for an extended period of time.

> *"...and I will **recompense them according to their deeds**, and **according** to the **works of their own hands**."* (Jeremiah 25:14)
>
> *"30) For we know him that hath said, Vengeance belongeth unto me, I will recompense, saith the Lord. And again, The Lord shall judge his people. 31) It is a **fearful thing to fall into the hands of the living God**."* (Hebrews 10:30-31)

Finally, we also need to remember that while all of the lost will be cast into the Lake of Fire, the very last reference to the "*second death*" in the Bible relates to those unfaithful Christians who were disobedient. Because they were not successful in being overcomers they: "***shall have their part in the lake which burneth with fire and brimstone:*** *which is* ***the second death.***" (Revelation 21:8)

These believers are not actually thrown into the Lake of Fire, but John says they will have their part in it. What this actually means is not known, but it does indicate these unfaithful Christians will be hurt by it (also please see: Revelation 2:11 and I Corinthians 3:15).

DEATH ABOLISHED

The Great White Throne Judgement period will last for 1,000 years (see pages 54-55). This will also be the Perfect Age where Jesus will reign over the new heaven and the new earth. One of His final acts will be putting an end to death itself:

> *"54) So when this corruptible has put on incorruption, and this mortal has put on immortality, then shall be brought to pass the saying that is written:* ***"Death is swallowed up in victory."*** *55)"O Death, where is your sting? O Hades, where is your victory?"*
> (I Corinthians 15:54-55 – NKJV)

> *"He will* ***swallow up death in victory;*** *and the Lord GOD will wipe away tears from off all faces; and the rebuke of his people shall he take away from off all the earth: for the LORD hath spoken it."* (Isaiah 25:8)

The very last enemy of mankind is death. Death came about because of disobedience and sin. The "*second death*" represents the cleansing of every trace of offense before a Holy God in the fiery lake of judgement in order to restore man.

The Lake of Fire will have served its purpose in bringing: *"the times of restitution of all things, which God hath spoken by the mouth of all his holy prophets since the world began."* (Acts 3:21). With death abolished, Jesus will have fully restored the world to that perfect state that existed before the fall of Adam.

REIGN RELINQUISHED

Once the Great White Throne Judgement period comes to a close, the **Perfect Age** will be complete. Jesus will then turn over His rule to God the Father.

> *"25) For He must reign till He has put all enemies under His feet. 26) The last enemy that will be destroyed is death. 27) For "He has put all things under His feet." But when He says "all things are put under Him," it is evident that He who put all things under Him is excepted. 28) Now when all things are made subject to Him, then* **the Son Himself will also be subject to Him** *who put all things under Him,* **that God may be all in all.***" (I Corinthians 15:25-28 – NKJV)

> *"3) And I heard a great voice out of heaven saying, Behold, the tabernacle of God is with men, and he will dwell with them, and they shall be his people,* **and God himself shall be with them**, *and be their God. 4) And God shall wipe away all tears from their eyes; and there shall be no more death, neither sorrow, nor crying, neither shall there be any more pain: for the former things are passed away."* (Revelation 21:3-4)

Once the judgement of mankind is completed, the very last enemy: death will be gone. Jesus will have completed His mission of restoring man to the condition that existed before the fall of Adam. God the Father will then take over at the end of the **Perfect Age** to be with man and be *"all in all."*

Chapter 7 – Beyond the Lake of Fire

Beyond the Lake of Fire, will be a wonderful and glorious time for all. The Perfect Age will be completed, and Jesus will turn over the reigns to God the Father. Jesus will have succeeded in the complete restoration of the world to the way it was before the fall in the Garden of Eden:

> *20) And he shall send Jesus Christ, which before was preached unto you: 21) Whom the heaven must receive until the **times of restitution of all things,** which God hath spoken by the mouth of all his holy prophets since the world began.* "(Acts 3:20-21)

CHRIST'S MISSION

It is important to remember what the mission was that God the Father gave to our Lord:

> *"For the Son of Man came to seek and to save (#4982) the lost."* (Luke 19:10 – ESV)

The Greek word for save in the above verse means to: save, deliver and to preserve. Our Lord's mission was to rescue all of mankind from the penalty of sin caused by the disobedience of man in the Garden. The Apostle John recorded the following regarding Christ's purpose:

> *38) "For I have come down from heaven, not to do My own will, but the will of Him who sent Me. 39) This is the will of the Father who sent Me, that of all He has given Me **I should lose nothing,** but **should raise it up at the last day."** (John 6:38-39 – NKJV)*

Here we see that Jesus was sent by His Father to raise everyone up at the "*last day*" which is referring to the 2nd Resurrection that takes place at the Great White Throne Judgement discussed in the previous chapters. Jesus indicates that He would "*lose nothing*" which signifies that our Lord will be successful in saving every single person leaving none behind. Everyone will be delivered and preserved because of Christ's success.

CHRIST'S VICTORY

Satan succeeded temporarily in causing all of mankind to face death. For approximately 6,000 years of human history, billions upon billions of people have gone to their graves. Jesus came to turn things around, and because of His victory everyone will receive the immortality that God originally intended:

> *"So when this **corruptible** has put on **incorruption**, and this **mortal** has put on **immortality**, then shall be brought to pass the saying that is written: "**Death is swallowed up in victory.**" 55) "O Death, where is your sting? O Hades, where is your victory? 56) The sting of death is sin, and the strength of sin is the law. 57) But thanks be to God, who gives us the **victory through our Lord Jesus Christ.**"* (I Corinthians 15:54-57 – NKJV)

When Jesus puts a complete end to death, all the mortal and corruptible elements of man will be destroyed. The Lake of Fire will have purged and purified all sin and disobedience from mankind putting incorruption and immortality upon everyone. Through the victory of our Lord Jesus Christ, man will be restored to the glorious estate that Adam and Eve enjoyed in the very beginning.

With disobedience, sin and death forever abolished; man will become the immortal beings God originally intended. With Christ's victory complete, He will surrender His reign to God the Father for all eternity. Jesus will have finished the work that was given to Him to do.

Epilogue

Now we see that Jesus will finish the work that was given for Him by His Father, the question remains: has the reader finished the work they were created to do? God has a purpose in creating every human being and He wants to see all flesh saved:

> **"And all flesh shall see the salvation of God."**
> (Luke 3:6 – NKJV)

Each reader needs to honestly answer the critical questions: *"Am I fulfilling the role, God created me for? Am I doing the work that He wanted me to do? Am I ready to meet Him if I were to die today or Christ returned tomorrow?"*

Hopefully this short book has helped the reader understand that God does love everyone and He wants to save all mankind:

> *"For God did not send His Son into the world to condemn the world, but that **the world through Him might be saved."*** (John 3:17 – NKJV)

It is our hearts' desire that this book will result in a countless number of people seeing God in an entirely new light. He wants everyone to be saved. The only remaining question is one of timing. Will you turn to Jesus now and receive Him as your Lord and Saviour? Or will you reject Him now, only to come before Him when you stand before the Great White Throne Judgement and face the Lake of Fire?

If you want to make sure you are ready to meet the Lord now, why not make the following prayer the prayer of your heart:

> *"Dear God in Heaven, I realize that I have not been living my life for you. I humbly turn to you right now and ask you to forgive me. Dear Jesus, please rule and reign in my heart and life. Please help me to live for you for whatever time remains. I pray that I may be able to escape all that is about to happen, and that I may be able to enter into your Kingdom when you return for me. In Jesus' name I pray. Amen"*

Our prayer is that many will pray this prayer and ask the Lord to help them be ready when Jesus comes to set-up His Kingdom.

> *"And now, little children, **abide in him**; that, when he shall appear, **we may have confidence**, and not be ashamed before him **at his coming**."* (I John 2:28)

> *"Beloved, now are we the sons of God, and it doth not yet appear what we shall be: but we know that, when he shall appear, we shall be like him; for we shall see him as he is. **And every man that hath this hope in him purifieth himself, even as he is pure.**"* (I John 3:2-3)

And let us never forget the prayer for watchfulness that our Lord instructed us to pray:

*"And take heed to yourselves, lest at any time your hearts be overcharged with surfeiting, and drunkenness, and cares of this life, and so that day come upon you unawares. For as a snare shall it come on all them that dwell on the face of the whole earth. **Watch ye, therefore, and pray always, that ye may be accounted worthy to escape all these things that shall come to pass, and to stand before the Son of man"** (Luke 21:34-36).*

Reference Notes

Prologue
1)   Source: www.tentmaker.org/tracts/Universalist.html
Chapter 1
2)   Bloomfield, Author – *How to Recognize the Antichrist*, Bethany Fellowship, Inc. © 1975, page 94
3)   Hanson, J.W. – ***Death, Resurrection, Immortality***, Concordant Publishing Concern, © 2001, page 78
4)   Beauchemin, Gerry with Reichard, D.Scott – *Hope Beyond Hell*, Malista Press, © 2010, p 194, www.HopeBeyondHell.net
Chapter 2
5)   Evely, Bob – *At The End of The Ages (The Abolition of Hell)*, Author House, © 2002, 2003 www.graceevangel.org and www.StudyShelf.com
6)   Dahl, Mikkel and Welker, Jon R. – *Is Hell Eternal?*, Shepherdsfileld Publishers, © 1984, 1996
7)   Hanson, J. W. – *Universalism In The Early Church*, Universalist Publishing House, © 1899, citation from Forewords – page x (book available at Google Books)
8)   Bauckham, Richard – **Universalism: A Historical Survey**, Theological Studies, © 1978, page 48 www.theologicalstudies.org.uk/article_universalism_bauckham
9)   Evely, ibid., page 108
10) Martin, Ernest L.– *Part 2 - The Recognition of Universal Reconciliation*, A.S.K.(Associates For Scriptural Knowledge). © 1982, 2002 www.askelm.com/doctrine/d020812.htm, page 3
11) Evely, ibid., page 117
12) Martin, ibid., page 4
13) Martin, ibid., page 4
14) Evely, ibid., page 123
15) Evely, ibid., page 120
16) Hanson, *Universalism In The Early Church*, page 260
17) Hanson, *Universalism In The Early Church*, page 19

Chapter 3
18) Hanson, J.W. – *AION – AIONIOS, Translated Everlasting – Eternal in the Holy Bible, Shown to Denote Limited Duration*, Concordant Publishing Concern, © 1875, 2001, p.73
19) Whipple, Gary T. – *Shock and Surprise Beyond The Rapture*, Schoettle Publishing Co., © 1992, pages 173 and 174. www.schoettlepublishing.com
20) Hanson, J.W. – *AION – AIONIOS, etc.* citation form the Preface
Appendix A
21) Larkin, Clarence – *Dispensational Truth*, Rev. Clarence Larkin Estate © 1918, P.O. Box 334, Glenside, PA 19038, U.S.A., 215-576-5590, *www.larkinestate.com*, page 77 ½
22) Hanson, J.W. – *AION – AIONIOS, etc.*, page 55
23) Mize, Lyn – *Eternal Life—Tradition vs. Scripture*, article located at: www.ffruits.org/firstfruits02/eternallife.html
The reader is encouraged to visit Lyn Mize' website for many more articles and exegesis of Scripture: www.ffruits.org
24) Todd, Grace H. – *Eonian Everlasting or Age-Lasting?*, Concordant Publishing Concern, page 18
25) Mize, Lyn – *The New Heaven & the New Earth*, exegesis located at: www.ffruits.org/firstfruits02/revchp2122.html

Other Recommended Books and Websites:
The following books and websites are highly recommended for those who want to learn more about the deeper Truths found in the Scriptures:

The Open Door
by Lyn Mize   www.ffruits.org
Worthy of the Kingdom
by Tom Finley   www.seekersofchrist.org
Judgment Seat of Christ
by D.M. Panton   www.schoettlepublishing.com
Kingdom, Power & Glory
by Nancy Missler   www.kingshighway.org
Rapture – A Reward for Readiness
by Dr. Ray Brubaker   www.godsnews.com

Appendix A – Questions and Answers

The above is just a sampling of some of the questions people have when they hear about the teaching in this book. If the reader has any additional questions that they would like to have answered, please feel free to send the author an e-mail or visit their website or send a letter to:

> e-mail: JimHarmanCPA@aol.com
> Website: www.ProphecyCountdown.com
> Address: P.O. Box 941612
>   Maitland, FL 32794

Q # 1 – Why is this teaching important?

A – The teaching of the *"glorious gospel"* that Jesus came to restore all of mankind is important for several reasons. First of all it reinstates the correct nature and character of God, as a God of love and compassion instead of a God that will punish mankind in pain and torment for all eternity. God's name is maligned by the teaching that He would eternally punish man and this could be corrected if the Church would come into a correct understanding of this issue. Secondly, this teaching would probably bring more people to Christ, because many are turned away by a Church that teaches eternal punishment. If this were changed, more souls would be saved and the Church would become a beacon for Christ. Finally, as Clarence Larkin points out in his book: **Dispensational Truth**, *"...That thus far Christianity, as a world converting power, is a failure..."*[21] He made this statement based upon a mathematical analysis of Church statistics and most theologians would probably agree with him. The failure of the Church to bring more people to Christ could partially be blamed on a doctrine that was not preached during the first 500 years of the Church.

Q # 2 – What about Hell? Is the Lake of Fire, "Hell"?

A – The subject of "hell" is misunderstood by many. The reader is encouraged to see our last book: **THE KINGDOM**, where an entire chapter is devoted to this complicated subject. It is a difficult subject because the Bible uses four words for hell and in 12 cases the word *"Gehenna"* was mistranslated as hell. Most of the confusion regarding hell in the New Testament has been caused by this error made by the translators. In Chapter 4, we discussed how the *"soul who sins...will die"* and the soul that dies goes to *sheol* or *hades*. This represents the "unseen" place where the soul goes at death. The Lake of Fire is not hell, but the place where all those in hades go to after their resurrection before the Great White Throne (2nd Resurrection).

It also should be remembered that during the Millennial Age the Lake of Fire is described as a place of torment (area of Dead Sea) for the unholy trio: the Antichrist and False Prophet (first 1,000 years) followed by Satan at the end of the Millennium. It is important to remember that after the Great White Throne Judgement, the Apostle John no longer describes the Lake of Fire as a place of torment. Also, with the renewal of a new heaven and new earth whether or not the Lake of Fire is relocated is not addressed by John.

Q # 3 – If punishment is not eternal, does that mean there is no eternal life either?

A – This is a popular argument when people first hear the teaching that punishment is not eternal. Rev. John Wesley Hanson tackles this question as follows:

> *"Then eternal life is not endless, for the same Greek adjective qualifies life and punishment."* This does not follow, for the word is used in Greek in different senses in the same sentence; as Habakkuk 3:6, "And the *everlasting* mountains were scattered – his ways are *everlasting*." Suppose we apply the popular argument here. The mountains and God must be of equal duration, for the same word is applied to both. Both are temporal or both are endless. But the mountains are expressly stated to be temporal – they "were scattered," – therefore God is not eternal. Or God is eternal and therefore the mountains must be…The argument does not hold water."[22]

Another aspect to the popular argument is the misunderstanding of what "eternal life" really is. Paul defines it as follows:

> *"6) He will render to each one according to his works: 7) to those who by patience in well-doing seek for glory and honor and immortality, he will give **eternal life**; 8) but for those who are self-seeking and do not obey the truth, but obey unrighteousness, there will be wrath and fury."* (Romans 2:6-8 – ESV)

The possession and duration of "*eternal life*" is dependent upon the person's fidelity and faithfulness. While "*eternal life*" is initially given to each believer, it can be forfeited by living a life of self-seeking and unrighteous living. The reader is encouraged to read an excellent article on this important subject entitled *Eternal Life—Tradition vs. Scripture* by Lyn Mize. [23]

Q # 4 – If everyone is going to be saved, then why even bother preaching the Gospel or going to Church?

A – Preaching the Gospel and going to Church are important for several reasons. The fact that God will eventually bring about the complete restoration of mankind is a message that should make the Church rejoice and bring added motivation to be even more diligent. People need Jesus in order to be saved now, because it would be far better to spend the next two Ages ruling and reigning with Christ than to be assigned to "*hades,*" "*outer darkness,*" or "*the Lake of Fire.*" Preaching the Gospel can help deliver many from these awful futures. Also, it was our Lord's last commands:

> *19) "Go therefore and **make disciples** of all the nations, baptizing them in the name of the Father and of the Son and of the Holy Spirit, 20) **teaching them** to observe all things that I have commanded you; and lo, I am with you always, even to the end of the age. "*
> (Matthew 28:19-20 – NKJV)

Jesus will be returning very, very soon, and the Church should be faithfully obeying His instructions.

Q # 5 – Aren't you teaching "heresy"?

A – According to Webster's dictionary, the definition of "heresy" is to "adhere to a religious opinion that is contrary to church dogma" and the "deviation from dominant theory, opinion or practice." Based upon this definition of "heresy," teaching Paul's "*Glorious Gospel*" that Jesus Christ will return to judge mankind for a limited period of time and then restore the world to that perfect state before the fall of Adam would be considered heretical. In my defense, however, I would charge that Augustine was equally as guilty as I am, for he was the chief architect of the "heretical" teaching of *eternal punishment*" that the Church has been plagued with since the first 500 years of Church history.

Q # 6 – Are there any other examples where the meanings of words were changed by the translators? How can I be sure which Bible is correct?

A – To answer the later part of the question first, we would encourage the reader to obtain an Interlinear Bible to use along with whichever version of the Bible that you prefer (King James, New KJ, English Standard Version, New International Version, etc.). Make sure the Interlinear Bible you purchase has the Strong's Concordance or you will have to buy it separately.

There have been several other examples how our Bibles have been changed over the years. In 1611, when the King James Bible was produced the translators changed the meaning of "*apostasia*" found in II Thessalonians 2:3, from "*departure*" or "*departing*" to "*falling away*." Up until this time, all of the previous translations used the correct meaning of "*departure*." The correct translations included: Spans 1384 to 1608, Wycliff 1384, Tyndale 1526, Coverdale 1535, Cranmer 1539, Breeches 1576, Beza 1583, Geneva 1608, and the Latin Vulgate in 400 A.D. Most subsequent translations have followed this error.

In 1885, more changes came about when the "Revised Version" (R.V.) came as a replacement for the Authorized King James Bible by the so called "textual critics" of that era! The R.V. altered Daniel 9:27 where Jesus Christ was changed to the Antichrist and the Apocrypha was removed after being part of the Bible for almost 2,000 years. (For more details on these changes please see our book: ***Don't Be Left Behind*** available at our website: www.ProphecyCountdown.com or at Amazon.

While the King James Bible is considered the most traditionally accepted bible to read, Joseph Kirk brings out a most startling discovery:

"...King James instructed the men who gave us the Authorized Version, 'To sanction no innovation that would disturb the orthodoxy or peace of the church.' What a vast difference it would have made in our thinking today had these translators followed consistently and accurately the Hebrew and Greek texts, instead of conforming to traditional teaching!"[24]

Had the translators been given different instructions, the Church and the world of today may have discovered that "*eternal punishment*" was a teaching of the dark ages.

Q # 7 – Why has God allowed this teaching to be hidden from the Church?

A – God has allowed this teaching to be hidden because He has given us freewill. Ever since Adam and Eve disobeyed the instructions they had been given, man has been given freedom to choose. The wise will be following the instructions Paul gave to Timothy: *"Study to shew thyself approved unto God, a workman that needeth not to be ashamed, rightly dividing the word of truth."* (II Timothy 2:15) Regardless what the world believes, every individual is going to be held accountable to God for what he believes and how that belief manifests itself in the person's life. God allows tests and trials in the world to refine and develop our character.

Q # 8 – This teaching sounds a little like what the Catholics call Purgatory? Please discuss.

A – Purgatory is the belief that one can either work out or pay for their sins in order to enter heaven or that others can pray people out of "purgatory." This false belief is nothing like the Lake of Fire. The Lake of Fire will be God's refining and purifying instrument for sinful and disobedient mankind. In the end, everyone will know Jesus as their Lord:

> *"10) That at the name of Jesus every knee should bow, of things in heaven, and things in earth, and things under the earth; 11) And that every tongue should* **confess that Jesus Christ is Lord**, *to the glory of God the Father."* (Philippians 2:10-11)

This will be the result of God purifying and refining each person because of His great love for man. It will be entirely because of God's grace and nothing else.

Q # 9 – What proof do you have that those hurt by the Lake of Fire are Christians?

A – This question relates to Revelation 21:5-8, which is a parenthetical statement in Chapter 21. While this chapter is dealing primarily with the New Jerusalem, the Apostle inserts a message dealing with the Church (see Page 57). In verse 7, Jesus says that all those who are overcomers will inherit all things. He then continues in verse 8, to describe all of those in the Church who are not overcomers. Because they failed in being overcomers it says they... *"***shall have their part in** *the* **lake of fire** *which burneth with fire and brimstone: which is the* **second death**.*" (Revelation 21:8) The fact that Christians will have a part in the lake of fire (which is the second death) is corroborated by Revelation 2:11:

> *"He that hath an ear, let him hear what the Spirit saith unto the churches; He that overcometh shall not be hurt of the* **second death**.*" (Revelation 2:11)

The usage of *"second death"* here relates to the Christians in the Church of Smyrna. John is warning the Church. He is saying that those who are *"overcomers"* will not be hurt by the *"second death."* By deduction, this is saying that those who are **not** *overcomers* will be **hurt by** the second death. For a more complete discussion regarding this important subject, please see our book: **THE KINGDOM** and the exegesis by Lyn Mize on the book of Revelation.[25]

Q # 10 – What part do works perform in relationship to a person's judgement?

A – Works play a part in the judgement of both Christians and non-Christians. Remember that Christians are saved completely by God's grace and works are not required: *"For by grace are ye saved through faith; and that not of yourselves: it is the gift of God: Not of works, lest any man should boast."* (Ephesians 2:8-9) While works will not save a person, they are still very important to God: *"For we are God's workmanship, created in Christ Jesus to **do good works**, which **God prepared in advance for us to do.**"* (Ephesians 2:10 – NIV) God will reward each Christian based upon their faithfulness in doing the good works which God wants them to do.

Likewise, non-Christians will also be judged by their works: *"And the sea gave up the dead which were in it; and death and hell delivered up the dead which were in them: and they were **judged** every man **according to their works.**"* (Revelation 20:13) Even though these individuals were not saved, they were judged based upon what they had done in this life. This indicates that the length and severity of the purification and chastisement process will vary from individual to individual. This agrees with the concept taught by the prophet Jeremiah: *"...and I will **recompense them according to their deeds**, and **according** to the **works of their own hands.**"* (Jeremiah 25:14)

How a person leads his life will play a big part in the reward or punishment that they receive. God is no respecter of persons (Acts 10:34) and every person will receive a just recompense of reward or punishment based upon their deeds and works they performed.

Q # 11 – Doesn't the story of Lazarus prove you are wrong?

A – No, the story of Lazarus is actually a parable. Please see Ernest L. Martin's excellent article that explains this important story in greater detail: www.askelm.com/doctrine/d030602.htm

Appendix B – Apocalypse of Peter

While we are including brief excerpts from *The Apocalypse of Peter* in this book, we do **not** believe it should be considered part of the word of God. As we have stated earlier, we believe that the Bible is the inspired word of God given to mankind to assist us in this life and to help us prepare for our afterlife. We believe it's important not to add or subtract from the Bible. But because this book was widely read during the early Church, we believe it is important for our readers to consider its teaching.

While *The Apocalypse of Peter* was not included in the final canon of Scripture, it was widely read during the first several hundred years of the Church. We have seen that the Early Church Fathers believed that God would ultimately bring about the restoration of all mankind which harmonizes with Peter's Apocalypse.

Over the years, there have been several bestselling books by authors who claim to have personally seen heaven and hell. We would ask the reader to decide if any of these books are any more credible than Peter's account?

It is important for the reader to understand that the terms, *"eternal," "everlasting"* and *"forever"* are used in *Peter's Apocalypse* in a similar manner that they are used in our Bibles today. As we have seen in this short study, these words would more properly have been translated as *"age lasting"* signifying the length would be for a limited duration. This is verified by the statements made in Chapters 13 and 14 where repentance is made and salvation finally given to everyone – with entrance into God's Kingdom by all.

Introduction to the *Apocalypse of Peter* by M.R. James

"We have not a pure and complete text of this book, which ranked next in popularity and probably also in date to the Canonical Apocalypse of St. John.

We have, first, certain quotations made by writers of the first four centuries.....Next, a fragment in Greek, called the Akhmim fragment, found with the Passion-fragment of the Gospel of Peter....(discovered in a tomb) now at Cairo. This is undoubtedly drawn from the Apocalypse of Peter....but my present belief is that,....it is part of the Gospel of Peter, which was a slightly later book than the Apocalypse...(the) Ethiopic version contained in one of the numerous forms of the books of Clement, a writing current in Arabic and Ethiopic....-dictated by Peter to Clement. The version of the Apocalypse contained in this has some extraneous matter at the beginning and the end; but, as I have tried to show in a series of articles in the Journal of Theological Studies (1910-11) and the Church Quarterly Review (1915), it affords the best general idea of the contents of the whole book which we have.

The second book of the Sibylline Oracles contains (in Greek hexameters) a paraphrase of a great part of the Apocalypse: and its influence can be traced in many early writings -the Acts of Thomas (55-57), the Martyrdom of Perpetua, the so-called Second Epistle of Clement, and, as I think, the Shepherd of Hermas: as well as in the Apocalypse of Paul and many later visions.

At one time (Peter's Apocalypse) was popular in Rome for the Muratorian Canon mentions it (late in the second century) along with the Apocalypse of John though it adds, that 'some will not have it read in the church.' The fifth-century church historian Sozomen (vii. 19) says that to his knowledge it was still read annually in some churches in Palestine on Good Friday."

THE ETHIOPIC TEXT

Chapter 1

"The Second Coming of Christ and Resurrection of the Dead (which Christ revealed unto Peter) who died because of their sins, for that they kept not the commandment of God their creator.

And he (Peter) pondered thereon, that he might perceive the mystery of the Son of God, the merciful and lover of mercy.

And when the Lord was seated upon the Mount of Olives, his disciples came unto him.

And we besought and entreated him severally and prayed him, saying unto him: Declare unto us what are the signs of thy coming and of the end of the world, that we may perceive and mark the time of thy coming and instruct them that come after us, unto whom we preach the word of thy gospel, and whom we set over (in) thy church, that they when they hear it may take heed to themselves and mark the time of thy coming.

And our Lord answered us, saying: Take heed that no man deceive you, and that ye be not doubters and serve other gods. Many shall come in my name, saying: I am the Christ. Believe them not, neither draw near unto them. For the coming of the Son of God shall not be plain (i.e. foreseen); but as the lightning that shineth from the east unto the west, so will I come upon the clouds of heaven with a great host in my majesty; with my cross going before my face will I come in my majesty, shining sevenfold more than the sun will I come in my majesty with all my saints, mine angels (mine holy angels). And my Father shall set a crown upon mine head, that I may judge the quick and the dead and **recompense every man according to his works**.

Chapter 2

And ye, take ye the likeness thereof (learn a parable) from the fig-tree: so soon as the shoot thereof is come forth and the twigs grown, the end of the world shall come.

And I, Peter, answered and said unto him: Interpret unto me concerning the fig-tree, whereby we shall perceive it; for throughout all its days doth the fig-tree send forth shoots, and every year it bringeth forth its fruit for its master. What then meaneth the parable of the fig-tree We know it not.

And the Master (Lord) answered and said unto me: Understandest thou not that the fig-tree is the house of Israel? Even as a man that planted a fig-tree in his garden, and it brought forth no fruit. And he sought the fruit thereof many years and when he found it not, he said to the keeper of his garden: Root up this fig-tree that it make not our ground to be unfruitful. And the gardener said unto God: (Suffer us) to rid it of weeds and dig the ground round about it and water it. If then it bear not fruit, we will straightway remove its roots out of the garden and plant another in place of it. Hast thou not understood that the fig-tree is the house of Israel? Verily I say unto thee, when the twigs thereof have sprouted forth in the last days, then shall feigned Christs come and awake expectation saying: I am the Christ, that am now come into the world. And when they (Israel) shall perceive the wickedness of their deeds they shall turn away after them and deny him [whom our fathers did praise], even the first Christ whom they crucified and therein sinned a great sin. But this deceiver is not the Christ. [something is wrong here: the sense required is that Israel perceives the wickedness of antichrist and does not follow him.] And when they reject him he shall slay with the sword, and there shall be many martyrs. Then shall the twigs of the fig-tree, that is, the house of Israel, shoot forth: many shall become martyrs at his hand. Enoch and Elias shall be sent to teach them that this is the deceiver which must come into the world and do signs and wonders to deceive. And therefore shall they that die by his hand be martyrs, and shall be reckoned among the good and righteous martyrs who have pleased God in their life. [Hermas, Vision III.i.9, speaks of 'those that have already been well-pleasing unto God and have suffered for the Name's sake'.]

Chapter 13

Thereafter shall the angels bring mine elect and righteous which are perfect in all uprightness, and bear them in their hands, and clothe them with the raiment of the life that is above.......

And all they that are in torment shall say with one voice: **Have mercy upon us, for now know we the judgement of God, which he declared unto us aforetime, and we believed not.** And the angel Tatirokos (Tartaruchus, keeper of hell: a word corresponding in formation to Temeluchus) shall come and chastise them with yet greater torment, and say unto them: Now do ye repent, when it is no longer the time for repentance, and naught of life remaineth. And they shall say: **Righteous is the judgement of God, for we have heard and perceived that his judgement is good; for we are recompensed according to our deeds.**

Chapter 14

Then will I **give** unto mine elect and righteous the washing (baptism) and the **salvation** for which **they** have **besought me**, in the field of Akrosja (Acherousia, a lake in other writings, e.g. Apocalypse of Moses -where the soul of Adam is washed in it: see also Paul 22, 23) which is called Aneslasleja (Elysium). **They shall adorn with flowers the portion of the righteous, and I shall go . . . I shall rejoice with them. I will cause the peoples to enter in to mine everlasting kingdom, and show**

them that eternal thing (life) whereon I have made them to set their hope, even I and my Father which is in heaven.

I have spoken this unto thee, Peter, and declared it unto thee. Go forth therefore and go unto the land (or city) of the west. (Duensing omits the next sentences as unintelligible; Grebaut and N. McLean render thus: and enter into the vineyard which I shall tell thee of, in order that by the sickness (sufferings) of the Son who is without sin **the deeds of corruption may be sanctified.** As for thee, thou art chosen according to the promise which I have given thee. **Spread thou therefore my gospel throughout all the world in peace. Verily men shall rejoice: my words shall be the source of hope and of life**, and suddenly shall the world be ravished.)

(We now have the section descriptive of paradise, which in the Akhmim text precedes that about hell.)

Chapter 15

And my Lord Jesus Christ our King said unto me: Let us go unto the holy mountain. And his disciples went with him, praying. And behold there were two men there, and we could not look upon their faces, for a light came from them, shining more than the sun, and their raiment also was shining, and cannot be described, and nothing is sufficient to be compared unto them in this world. And the sweetness of them . . . that no mouth is able to utter the beauty of their appearance (or, the mouth hath not sweetness to express, &c.), for their aspect was astonishing and wonderful. And the other, great, I say (probably: and, in a word, I cannot describe it), shineth in his (sic) aspect above crystal. Like the flower of roses is the appearance of the color of his aspect and of his body . . . his head (al. their head was a marvel). And upon his (their) shoulders (evidently something about their hair has dropped out) and on their foreheads was a crown of nard woven of fair flowers. As the rainbow in the water, [Probably: in the time of rain. From the LXX of Ezek.i.28.] so was their hair. And such was the comeliness of their countenance, adorned with all manner of ornament.

Chapter 16

And when we saw them on a sudden, we marveled. And I drew near unto the Lord (God) Jesus Christ and said unto him: O my Lord, who are these And he said unto me: They are Moses and Elias. And I said unto him: (Where then are) Abraham and Isaac and Jacob and the rest of the righteous fathers? And he showed us a great garden, open, full of fair trees and blessed fruits, and of the odour of perfumes. The fragrance thereof was pleasant and came even unto us. And thereof (al. of that tree) . . . saw I much fruit. And my Lord and God Jesus Christ said unto me: Hast thou seen the companies of the fathers.

As is their rest, such also is the honour and the glory of them that are persecuted for my righteousness' sake. And I rejoiced and believed [and believed] and understood that which is written in the book of my Lord Jesus Christ. And I said unto him: O my Lord, wilt thou that I make here three tabernacles, one for thee, and one for Moses, and one for Elias? And he said unto me in wrath: Satan maketh war against thee, and hath veiled thine understanding; and the good things of this world prevail against thee. Thine eyes therefore must be opened and thine ears unstopped that a tabernacle, not made with men's hands, which my heavenly Father hath made for me and for the elect. And we beheld it and were full of gladness.

Chapter 17

And behold, suddenly there came a voice from heaven, saying: This is my beloved Son in whom I am well pleased: (He has kept) my commandments. And then came a great and exceeding white cloud over our heads and bare away our Lord and Moses and Elias. And I trembled and was afraid: and we looked up and the heaven opened and we beheld men in the flesh, and they came and greeted our Lord and Moses and Elias and went into another heaven. And the word of the scripture was fulfilled: This is the generation that seeketh him and seeketh the face of the God of Jacob. And great fear and commotion was there in heaven and the angels pressed one upon another that the word of the scripture might be fulfilled which saith: Open the gates, ye princes.

Thereafter was the heaven shut, that had been open.

And we prayed and went down from the mountain, glorifying God, which hath written the names of the righteous in heaven in the book of life."

From *"The Apocryphal New Testament"* – M.R. James Translation and Notes Oxford: Clarendon Press, 1924

The above excerpts that are included in this Appendix came from **The Apocalypse of Peter** which can be found at the following link accessed 12/4/2010:

URL (http://wesley.nnu.edu/sermons-essays-books/noncanonical-literature/apocalypse-of-peter)

Permission to quote was freely granted by the Wesley Center Online at Northwest Nazarene University, 623 Holly Street Nampa, ID 83686. Note: Chapter numbers have been added in order to help facilitate comparison with versions by other sources. Words in bold emphasis are authors in order to stress important ideas and concepts relating to the subject of this book.

Appendix C – Age vs. World

As outlined in Chapter 3, the translation of the Greek words *aion* and *aionias* have caused much confusion. This brief appendix will illustrate how the King James translation using the word *world* would be clearer if the word **age** is used:

Matthew 12:32

*And whosoever speaketh a word against the Son of man, it shall be forgiven him: but whosoever speaketh against the Holy Ghost, it shall not be forgiven him, neither in this **world**, neither in the **world** to come. (KJ)*

*And whoever speaks a word against the Son of Man will be forgiven, but whoever speaks against the Holy Spirit will not be forgiven, either in this **age** or in the **age** to come. (ESV)*

Matthew 13:39-40

*39) The enemy that sowed them is the devil; the harvest is the end of the **world**; and the reapers are the angels. 40) As therefore the tares are gathered and burned in the fire; so shall it be in the end of this **world**. (KJ)*

*39) and the enemy who sowed them is the devil. The harvest is the close of the **age**, and the reapers are angels 40) Just as the weeds are gathered and burned with fire, so will it be at the close of the **age**. (ESV)*

Matthew 24:3

*And as he sat upon the mount of Olives, the disciples came unto him privately, saying, Tell us, when shall these things be? and what [shall be] the sign of thy coming, and of the end of the **world**? (KJ)*

*As he sat on the Mount of Olives, the disciples came to him privately, saying, "Tell us, when will these things be, and what will be the sign of your coming and of the close of the **age**?" (ESV)*

Mark 10:30
But he shall receive an hundredfold now in this time, houses, and brethren, and sisters, and mothers, and children, and lands, with persecutions; and in the world to come eternal life. (KJ)
Who will not receive a hundredfold now in this time, houses and brothers and sisters and mothers and children and lands, with persecutions, and in the age to come eternal life. (ESV)

Luke 20:34-35
34) *And Jesus answering said unto them, The children of this world marry, and are given in marriage: 35) But they which shall be accounted worthy to obtain that world, and the resurrection from the dead, neither marry, nor are given in marriage:* (KJ)
34) *And Jesus said to them, "The sons of this age marry and are given in marriage, 35) but those who are considered worthy to attain to that age and to the resurrection from the dead neither marry nor are given in marriage,* (ESV)

Galatians 1:4
Who gave himself for our sins, that he might deliver us from this present evil world, according to the will of God and our Father: (KJ)
Who gave himself for our sins to deliver us from the present evil age, according to the will of our God and Father, (ESV)

II Timothy 4:10
For Demas hath forsaken me, having loved this present world, and is departed unto Thessalonica; Crescens to Galatia, Titus unto Dalmatia. (KJ)
For Demas forsook me, having loved the present age, and went on to Thessalonica, Crescens to Galatia, Titus to Dalmatia, (YLT)

The reader may also be interested in reading Hebrews 6:5 and Revelation 20:10 to see the distinction of the words there also.

Appendix D

Sign of Christ's Coming

April 8, 1997

Comet Hale-Bopp Over New York City
Credit and Copyright: J. Sivo
http://antwrp.gsfc.nasa.gov/apod/ap970408.html

"What's that point of light above the World Trade Center? It's Comet Hale-Bopp! Both faster than a speeding bullet and able to "leap" tall buildings in its single <u>orbit</u>, Comet Hale-Bopp is also bright enough to be seen even over the glowing lights of one of the world's premier cities. In the foreground lies the East River, while much of New York City's Lower Manhattan can be seen between the river and the comet."

- -

"As it was in the days of Noah, so it will be at the coming of the Son of Man." (Matthew 24:37 – NIV)

These words from our wonderful Lord have several applications about the Tribulation period that is about to ensnare this world.

Seas Lifted Up
Throughout the Old Testament, the time of the coming Tribulation period is described as the time when the "seas have lifted up," and also as coming in as a "flood" (please see Jeremiah 51:42, Hosea 5:10, Daniel 11:40 and Psalm 93:3-4 for just a few examples).

This is a direct parallel to the time of Noah when the Great Flood of water came to wipe out every living creature except for righteous Noah and his family, and the pairs of animals God spared. While God said He would never flood the earth again with water, the coming Judgement will be by fire (II Peter 3:10). The book of Revelation shows that approximately three billion people will perish in the terrible time that lies ahead (see Revelation 6:8 and 9:15).

2 Witnesses
A guiding principle of God is to establish a matter based upon the witness of two or more:

> *"...a matter must be established by the testimony of two or three witnesses"* (Deuteronomy 19:15 – NIV)

In 1994, God was able to get the attention of mankind when Comet Shoemaker-Levy crashed into Jupiter on the 9th of Av (on the Jewish calendar). Interestingly, this Comet was named after the "two" witnesses who first discovered it.

In 1995, "two" more astronomers also discovered another comet. It was called Comet Hale-Bopp, and it reached its closest approach to planet Earth on March 23, 1997. It has been labeled as the most widely viewed comet in the history of mankind.

Scientists have determined that Comet Hale-Bopp's orbit brought it to our solar system 4,465 years ago (see Notes 1 and 2 below). In other words, the comet made its appearance near Earth in 1997 and also in 2468 BC. Remarkably, this comet preceded the Great Flood by 120 years! God warned Noah of this in Genesis 6:3:

> *"My Spirit shall not strive with man forever, for he is indeed flesh; yet his days shall be one hundred and twenty years."*

Days of Noah
What does all of this have to do with the Lord's return? Noah was born around 2948 BC, and Genesis 7:11, tells us that the Flood took place when Noah was 600, or in 2348 BC.

Remember, our Lord told us: ***"As it was in the days of Noah, so it will be at the coming of the Son of Man."*** (Matthew 24:37 – NIV)

In the original Greek, it is saying: ***"exactly like"*** it was, so it will be when He comes (see Strong's #5618).

During the days of Noah, Comet Hale-Bopp arrived on the scene as a harbinger of the Great Flood. Just as this same comet appeared before the Flood, could its arrival again in 1997 be a sign that God's final Judgement, also known as the time of Jacob's Trouble, is about to begin?

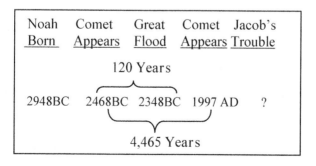

Comet Hale-Bopp's arrived 120 years before the Flood as a warning to mankind. Only righteous Noah heeded God's warning and built the ark, as God instructed. By faith, Noah was obedient to God and, as a result, saved himself and his family from destruction.

Remember, Jesus told us His return would be preceded by great heavenly signs: *"And there shall be signs in the sun, and in the moon, and in the stars; and upon the earth distress of nations, with perplexity; the sea and the waves roaring..."* (Luke 21:25)

Just as this large comet appeared as a 120-year warning to Noah, its arrival in 1997 tells us that Jesus is getting ready to return again. Is this the **"Sign"** Jesus referred to?

Jesus was asked 3 questions by the disciples:
"Tell us, (1) when shall these things be" (the destruction of the city of Jerusalem), *" and (2) what shall be the __sign__ of thy coming, and (3) of the end of the world?"* (Matthew 24:3)

Sign of Christ's Coming

The **first** question had to do with events that were fulfilled in 70 AD. The **third** question has to do with the future time at the very end of the age.

The **second** question, however, has to do with the time of Christ's second coming. Jesus answered this second question in His description of the days of Noah found in Matthew 24:33-39:

(33) *"So likewise ye, when ye shall see all these things, know that it is near, even at the doors. (34) Verily I say unto you, This generation shall not pass, till all these things be fulfilled. (35) Heaven and earth shall pass away, but my words shall not pass away. (36) But of that day and hour knoweth no man, no, not the angels of heaven, but my Father only. (37) **But as the days of Noe were, so shall also the coming of the Son***

of man be. *(38)For as in the days that were before the flood they were eating and drinking, marrying and giving in marriage, until the day that Noe entered into the ark, (39) And knew not until the flood came, and took them all away; so shall also the coming of the Son of man be."*

Jesus is telling us that the **_sign_** of His coming will be as it was during the days of Noah. As Comet Hale-Bopp was a sign to the people in Noah's day, its arrival in 1997 is a sign that Jesus is coming back again soon. Comet Hale-Bopp could be the very sign Jesus was referring to, which would announce His return for His faithful.

Remember, Jesus said, *"**exactly as** it was in the days of Noah, so will it be when He returns."* The appearance of Comet Hale-Bopp in 1997 is a strong indication that the Tribulation period is about to begin, but before then, Jesus is coming for His Bride!

Keep looking up! Jesus is coming again very soon!
As Noah prepared for the destruction God warned him about 120 years before the Flood, Jesus has given mankind a final warning that the Tribulation period is about to begin. The horrible destruction on 9/11 is only a precursor of what is about to take place on planet Earth. We need to be wise like Noah and prepare. Always remember our Lord's instructions:

Watch and Pray
*"(34)And take heed to yourselves, lest at any time your hearts be overcharged with surfeiting, and drunkenness, and cares of this life, and so that day come upon you unawares. (35) For as a snare shall it come on all them that dwell on the face of the whole earth.(36)**Watch ye therefore, and pray always, that ye may be accounted worthy to escape all these things that shall come to pass, and to stand before the Son of man"** (Luke 21:34-36).

Footnotes

(1) The original orbit of Comet Hale-Bopp was calculated to be approximately 265 years by engineer George Sanctuary in his article: *Three Craters In Israel*, published on March 31, 2001 that can be found at: http://www.gsanctuary.com/3craters.html#3c_r13

Comet Hale-Bopp's orbit around the time of the Flood changed from 265 years to about 4,200 years. Because the plane of the comet's orbit is perpendicular to the earth's orbital plane (ecliptic), Mr. Sanctuary noted: "A negative time increment was used for this simulation…to back the comet away from the earth…. past Jupiter… and then out of the solar system. The simulation suggests that the past-past orbit had a very eccentric orbit with a period of only 265 years. When the comet passed Jupiter (*around 2203BC)* its orbit was deflected upward, coming down near the earth 15 months later with the comet's period changed from 265 years to about (*4,200)* years." (*added text for clarity*)

(2) Don Yeomans, with NASA's Jet Propulsion Laboratory made the following observations regarding the comet's orbit: "By integrating the above orbit forward and backward in time until the comet leaves the planetary system and then referring the osculating orbital elements…the following orbital periods result: Original orbital period before entering planetary system = 4200 years. Future orbital period after exiting planetary system = 2380 years."
This analysis can be found at: http://www2.jpl.nasa.gov/comet/ephemjpl6.html

Based upon the above two calculations we have the following:

265 [a] + 4,200 [b] = 4,465 Years

1997 AD – 4,465 Years = 2468 BC = Hale Bopp arrived

(a) Orbit period calculated by George Sanctuary before deflection around 2203 BC.

(b) Orbit period calculated by Don Yeomans after 1997 visit.

Special Invitation

This book hopes to bring people to a better knowledge of Jesus Christ. If you have never been saved before, would you like to be saved? The Bible shows that it's simple to be saved...

- Realize you are a sinner.
  "As it is written, There is none righteous, no, not one:"
  (Romans 3:10)
  "... for there is no difference. For all have sinned, and come short of the glory of God;" (Romans 3:22-23)
- Realize you CAN NOT save yourself.
  "But we are all as an unclean thing, and all our righteousness are as filthy rags; ..." (Isaiah 64:6)
  "Not by works of righteousness which we have done, but according to his mercy he saved us, ..." (Titus 3:5)
- Realize that Jesus Christ died on the cross to pay for your sins.
  "Who his own self bare our sins in his own body on the tree, ..." (I Peter 2:24)
  "... Unto him that loved us, and washed us from our sins in his own blood," (Revelation 1:5)
- Simply by faith receive Jesus Christ as your personal Savior.
  "But as many as received him, to them gave he power to become the sons of God, even to them that believe on his name:" (John 1:12)
  " ...Sirs, what must I do to be saved? And they said, Believe on the Lord Jesus Christ, and thou shalt be saved, and thy house." (Acts 16:30-31)
  "...if you confess with your mouth, 'Jesus is Lord,' and believe in your heart God raised him from the dead, you will be saved." (Romans 10:9 – NIV)

WOULD YOU LIKE TO BE SAVED?

If you want to be saved, you can receive Jesus Christ right now by making the following confession of faith:

> Lord Jesus, I know that I am a sinner, and unless you save me, I am lost. I thank you for dying for me at Calvary. By faith I come to you now, Lord, the best way I know how, and ask you to save me. I believe that God raised you from the dead and acknowledge you as my personal Saviour.

If you believed on the Lord, this is the most important decision of your life. You are now saved by the precious blood of Jesus Christ, which was shed for you and your sins. Now that you have received Jesus as your personal Saviour, you will want to find a Church where you can be baptized as your first act of obedience, and where the word of God is taught so you can continue to grow in your faith. Ask the Holy Spirit to help you as you read the Bible to learn all that God has for your life.

Also, go to the Reference section of this book where you will find recommended books and websites that will help you on your wonderful journey.

Endtimes
The Bible indicates that we are living in the final days and Jesus Christ is getting ready to return very soon. This book was written to help people prepare for what lies ahead. The word of God indicates that the Tribulation Period is rapidly approaching and that the Antichrist is getting ready to emerge on the world scene.

Jesus promised His disciples that there is a way to escape the horrible time of testing and persecution that will soon devastate this planet. One of the purposes of this book is to help you get prepared so you will be ready when Jesus Christ returns.

About The Author

Jim Harman has been a Christian for over 31 years. He has diligently studied the word of God with a particular emphasis on Prophecy. Jim has written several books and the four most essential titles are available at www.ProphecyCountdown.com: *The Coming Spiritual Earthquake, Don't Be Left Behind, The Kingdom, and Beyond the Lake of Fire;* which have been widely distributed around the world. These books encourage many to continue *"Looking"* for the Lord's soon return, and bring many to a saving knowledge of Jesus Christ.

Jim's professional experience includes being a Certified Public Accountant (CPA) and a Certified Property Manager (CPM). He has an extensive background in both public accounting and financial management with several well known national firms.

Jim has been fortunate to have been acquainted with several mature believers who understand and teach the deeper truths of the Bible. It is Jim's strong desire that many will come to realize the importance of seeking the Kingdom and seeking Christ's righteousness as we approach the soon return of our Lord and Saviour Jesus Christ.

The burden of his heart is to see many come to know the joy of Christ's triumph in their life as they become true overcomers; qualified and ready to rule and reign with Christ in the coming Kingdom.

To contact the author for questions or to arrange for speaking engagements:

Jim Harman
P.O. Box 941612
Maitland, FL 32794
JimHarmanCPA@aol.com

Reader's Comments

Any true Christian who reads of the unfathomable Love and Mercy of our Precious God and Father of Our Lord Jesus Christ and rejects it as heresy....his love of God is too shallow. How could any of us who have had the LOVE of GOD shed abroad in our heart for His fallen World enjoy Heaven to the fullest...knowing the great bulk of Humanity, never having a second chance, are burning forever in hell somewhere in the Universe??? FATHER, enlarge our hearts vision and Love for You...we're so grateful... "Your ways are higher than our ways."   Joan Olsen – Edmond, OK

Jim was the first person to help me think "outside of the box" to traditional church thinking. Jim has again done his homework and has given us a dear Truth that is so important to know, that God will bring everything back into himself, so He *may be all in all*. It helps us as believers to see why we are to love everyone, Arabs, Jews, atheists, and even the enemy. We have forgotten how to be humble (teachable) as in James 4:10 and in 1 Peter 5:6. These are promises but we have to do our part. May we all do so in these end days before it is too late. Thanks again, Jim, for helping us learn more of His precious Truth.
                              Robin Wade – Ft. Pierce, FL

Even though I am "Concordant" in my understanding of the Scriptures, and might understand some things differently, this book is an excellent work that I will be sharing with other Truth seekers. It is presented in an easy to read and follow format – making it a great study tool, especially for common folk like myself. The subject of the Lake Of Fire has always been one of my favorite topics of study and this book brings forward Scripture verses that highlight the Glorious Gospel of Jesus Christ. I highly recommend it to all who read the Scriptures and have or had questions regarding what some have considered an uncomfortable topic.   Bruce De Vrou – Grand Rapids, MI

Reader's Comments

The Salvation of all is a message that has been tragically lost to traditional Christian churches. This book does a wonderful job in showing what the early Christians believed and how Augustine was used by the Adversary to change that message. I fully agree the Scripture teaches that all will be Saved and Reconciled to God and our Lord Jesus will succeed in doing what the Scripture says He came to do – "to seek and to save the lost" (Luke 19:10). Although I may not agree with some of the conclusions in your books regarding the details, I support the message that in the end of the ages, everyone will have been saved, justified and reconciled - all to the glory of God.

Robert Lakey – Sayre, OK

Well Brother Harman, you have done it again. You have nailed down another particularly controversial topic which the church at large should be forced to address. Your words run in direct opposition to that which is taught in the corporate church today. The shepherds of the flock have failed to teach the truth of the phrase *"that God may be all in all"* found in 1 Corinthians 15:28, AND have danced all around the *"fire"* that even the carnal Christian may need to endure to bring the necessary cleansing to prepare him for that end. Thank you for your splendid work on the subject and your clear presentation of a truth that is long overdue to the body of Christ.

Karen Bishop – Glasgow, KY

All of my life I wondered how such a loving God could punish people with *"eternal torment."* I particularly could not understand how a person who lived in a remote part of the world who never even heard the good news about Jesus Christ dying for them would be sentenced to punishment in hell forever. Thank you so much Jim for your boldness in writing this wonderful book; it helps to know that God will ultimately restore everyone because of His wonderful grace, love and mercy for all of mankind.   John David – St. Louis, MO

Reader's Comments

If you have ever had to sit through the funeral of an unbeliever, it can be traumatic to say the least. Jim's book casts light and hope beyond where the Preacher may have left things with the grieving family and makes a case for the complete and utter Restoration for everyone and everything. You may be utterly surprised to learn that this glorious message anchored our church fathers for the first 500 years after Christ's ascension. My whole life I was taught that God is Love, yet I never could reconcile a place of *eternal torment* for the majority of His creation no matter how many ways it was explained to me. The Truths presented in this book are like a basket of hope filled with life giving revelation. You will see that His plan is to one day bring us all Home and He will indeed do all He has purposed to do because nothing is impossible for Him.

Pamalia R. Culvern – Madison, GA

To read a book about the All Encompassing Love of God is a breath of fresh air. God's ultimate plan of the ages is to bring humanity back to Himself (Acts 3:20-21). Thank God for Jim's book which proves God's redemption plan is greater than Adam's ability to bring the human race down.

Pastor Mike Cronk – Peculiar, MO
Joyful Sound Worship Center

Reader's Comments

Not all comments were as encouraging as those included above. The following comment came from a brother in the Lord whose name is being withheld for obvious reasons:

I have not had the time to review the draft copy of your new book. I do feel that I should caution you on publishing this topic without first considering the following: (1) Your thesis denying eternal punishment is a denial of a significant doctrine of the faith, not a minor one. The fact that almost no evangelical theologians support this should give you pause. (2) Please realize that if you are wrong, God will call you to account – especially for the possibility that some might downplay – through your influence – the need for salvation or witnessing to the lost. The souls of men are at stake.

Anonymous

The author appreciates this brother's concern; but encourages him, as well as any others who hold similar views, to please take the time to at least read this book. While "*eternal punishment*" is a sacred doctrine for most of the Church, this book uncovers how one man was used by the Adversary to blind mankind from the "*glorious gospel*" that Jesus came to provide. The message of this book is that salvation and witnessing remain **vital ingredients** in fulfilling the great commission that our Lord commanded us to perform. With a proper understanding of what the "*glorious gospel*" really is, the Church could be energized to proclaim the **really, really good news** that Jesus Christ came to save the entire world. By witnessing and proclaiming this wonderful news, the Church could be even more successful in rescuing more of mankind from an encounter with the lake of fire.

'Twas the Night Before Jesus Came

'Twas the night before Jesus Came and all through the house
    Not a creature was praying, not one in the house.
Their Bibles were lain on the self without care
    In hopes that Jesus would not come there.
The children were dressing to crawl into bed,
    Not once ever kneeling or bowing a head.
And Mom in her rocker with baby on her lap
    Was watching the Late Show while I took a nap.
When out of the East there arose such a clatter,
    I sprang to my feet to see what was the matter.
Away to the window I flew like a flash
    Tore open the shutters and threw up the sash!
When what to my wondering eyes should appear
    But angels proclaiming that Jesus was here
With a light like the sun sending forth a bright ray
    I knew in a moment this must be The Day!
The light of His face made me cover my head
    It was Jesus! Returning just like He had said.
And though I possessed worldly wisdom and wealth,
    I cried when I saw Him in spite of myself.
In the Book of Life which He held in His hand,
    Was written the name of every saved man.
He spoke not a word as He searched for my name;
    When He said "It's not here" my head hung in shame.
The people whose names had been written with love
    He gathered to take to His Father above.
With those who were ready He rose without a sound
    While all the rest were left standing around.
I fell to my knees, but it was too late;
    I had waited too long and thus sealed my fate.
I stood and I cried as they rose out of sight;
    Oh, if only I had been ready tonight.
In the words of this poem the meaning is clear;
    The coming of Jesus is drawing near.
There's only one life and when comes the last call
    We'll find that the Bible was true after all!

HELP DISTRIBUTE THIS MESSAGE

Prophecy Countdown Publications does not have the resources to distribute this important message to all the bookstores so this PDF book is being made available to everyone free of charge at: www.ProphecyCountdown.com. Copy this PDF file to your computer and e-mail to all those who you care about.

"The end of the age is coming soon. Therefore be earnest, thoughtful men of prayer."
(I Peter 4:7 – Paraphrase)

Is Daniel's Clock about to Start Ticking once again?
The recovery of the Old City of Jerusalem in June 1967 was a pivotal
Prophetic Event. Find out how this major Prophetic Milestone may
correlate with the start of the Second Half of Daniel's 70th Week.

> See to it that no one takes you captive through hollow and
> deceptive philosophy, which depends on human tradition and
> the basic principles of this world rather than on Christ.
> (Colossians 2:8 NIV)

The "Traditional" teaching on the "70th Week of Daniel" has taken
the Church captive into believing almost a "fairy tale" regarding
Endtime events. Find out the beautiful Truth that has been hidden
from modern day Christians.

MUST READING FOR EVERY CHRISTIAN

Jesus Christ is returning for His Bride. Are you "Watching" for your
Bridegroom today? Find out the consequences of not being ready
before the final grains of sand descend through the hour glass. Don't
be one of those who will be LEFT BEHIND!

Order your copy today from www.ProphecyCountdown.com

Or from Amazon.com – Available in Paperback and or Kindle Edition

Once a person is saved, the number one priority should be seeking entrance into the Kingdom through the salvation of their soul. It is pictured as a runner in a race seeking a prize represented by a crown that will last forever.

The salvation of the soul and entrance into the coming Kingdom are only achieved through much testing and the trial of one's faith. If you are going through difficulty, then REJOICE:

> *"Blessed is the man who perseveres under trial, because when he has stood the test, he will receive the crown of life that God has promised to those who love Him."* (James 1:12)

The "Traditional" teaching on the "THE KINGDOM" has taken the Church captive into believing all Christians will rule and reign with Christ no matter if they have lived faithful and obedient lives, or if they have been slothful and disobedient with the talents God has given them. Find out the important Truth before Jesus Christ returns.

MUST READING FOR EVERY CHRISTIAN

Jesus Christ is returning for His faithful overcoming followers. Don't miss the opportunity of ruling and reigning with Christ in the coming KINGDOM!

Download your FREE copy: www.ProphecyCountdown.com

The Day of the Lord is Near!

The Coming Spiritual Earthquake

by James T. Harman

"The Message presented in this book is greatly needed to awaken believers to the false ideas many have when it comes to the Rapture. I might have titled it: THE RAPTURE EARTH-QUAKE!"
Ray Brubaker - God's News Behind the News

"If I am wrong, anyone who follows the directions given in this book will be better off spiritually. If I am right, they will be among the few to escape the greatest spiritual calamity of the ages."
Jim Harman - Author

MUST READING FOR EVERY CHRISTIAN!
HURRY! BEFORE IT IS TOO LATE!

CPSIA information can be obtained at www.ICGtesting.com
Printed in the USA
BVOW08s0554220615

405041BV00002B/108/P